LET'S EATT

PRESS

Editing by Selena Hostetler
Cover and book design by Karen Cantu

10 9 8 7 6 5 4 3 2 1
ISBN: 978-1-961935-00-6

Dr. Michael Séan Mills

Arise, Mighty Army:

Trinitarian Discipleship, T3D International

Forwards by Dr. David Ramirez, Third Assistant General Overseer for the Church of God, Cleveland, TN and Dr. Don Ross, Team Leader, NWMN

Endorsements

"

"After 42 years of ministry in the local church, organizational/ administrative leadership, coaching, and mentoring, I am often asked, "What is the greatest need of the church?" My answer is simple and quick, "Discipleship. Training the body of Christ how to grow spiritually and then, in turn, train others." My dear friend, Dr. Michael Mills, in his excellent work, Arise, Mighty Army: Trinitarian Discipleship, T3D International, has developed an incredible tool to fulfill the need of the hour. His systematic approach has diffused the mystery of how-to disciple others. The unique approach of combining evangelism and discipleship is refreshing. While many try to complicate the methodology of developing others, Dr. Mills provides a theological approach with a practical and simplistic plan that transcends cultures. This work is not a work of theory only. Dr. Mills presents an incredible lesson plan and an example of a Social/Evangelistic Project to aid in facilitating and developing an Army of Warriors! Dr. Mills has created a tool that will not only grow the local church but will also increase the Kingdom of God."

Dr. Derwood L. Perkins, PhD
Mississippi Administrative Bishop (for the entire State)
Church of God, Cleveland, TN

"

Over several years, I have watched Michael & Denise Mills as they have lived out their faith on the Mission field. I am delighted that in this book Michael brings us back to the heart, and nature, of the Triune God. Discipleship must reflect the fellowship and relationship that exists in God."

Nick Park
Senior Pastor, Solid Rock, National Overseer, Church of God Ireland.
Executive Director, Evangelical Alliance Ireland.

We joined Church of God in 1995. I was 33 years old. We had 3 churches in Ireland and a grand total of 50 members. Now I'm 60, and we have 32 churches with 3,500 members. God is good.

66

This is an exceptional book that does not deal in theory alone, but also deals with practical applications of making disciples. There is no doubt that this will be a life-changing, kingdom-building book."

Pastor Dwight Allen,
Turnaround, Grassroots Lead Pastor
St. Augustine Church of God, 5 years
Zephyrhills COG, 7 years
Cooper City COG, 31 years
The Anchor COG, 6 years (current)

66

This heart-changing material cuts through the lie of the world's teaching about the power of mindset to reveal our deep need, desire, and petition for a heart after God's own heart. This book leverages knowledge and reason to keep mind (Gnosis) and heart (Yada) together to strengthen readers in God's Spirit."

"By faith in Christ, our daily submission to His counseling will lead us rightly and urgently to discipleship for Christ. This book convicts a leader's heart to get out of the pews, stand firmly, and intentionally bring others to the feet of the King of Kings."

Priscila Caceres
Slovakian church thinker

In Memory Of

This book is in memory of my precious soulmate, Denise. Of course, after 42 years of marriage, I called her Niser. She was an incredible woman of God, wife, mother, and grandmother! My son Sean, daughter Bryana, and grandson Aaronn would agree with me on that point.

If you are married, you know that if one person accomplishes a doctorate, both have done the work. I gave Niser a gift to let her know that I appreciated her help with my doctorate. I also asked her, now that she had helped me complete my work, what she would like to accomplish in her personal life.

Niser told me that she would like to earn a chef's degree. I gave my all to help her accomplish her three-year goal. Her cooking was amazing! She was such a great chef that she destroyed a few of my favorite places to eat out. Her food was that much better! She inspired me to write my first proverb, Mills 1:1, "It is a wise man who sends his wife to culinary school."

A few years later, I came to Niser and said that I felt like I should work on another doctorate. She told me that she did not feel the same. I asked her what she wanted to see me doing. She told me that she wanted me to write a book!

My soulmate gave her life during covid here in Ecuador. We had been living here for 31 years when she gave her life to the Lord and the people of Ecuador. The fulfillment of my word to my precious wife is this book in your hands: *Arise, Mighty Army: Trinitarian Discipleship.*

I know that she would have been proud of me. She would have been thrilled to see the Lord moving to empower this program for making disciples across the globe. This book is for the Lord, for you my sweet, and for all of you wanting to learn "how" to make disciples.

My Thanks to Him:

I want to thank the Trinity for entrusting me with this incredible discipleship program. In addition to giving me the T3D study material, the Trinity also enabled me to teach it on 4 continents and helped me write the book that you are now reading. My prayer is that the Trinity will fill your life and help you be involved in this active movement. This movement is a resurgence of what Jesus started in the New Testament: making disciples!

Table of Contents

Forewords by Dr. David Ramirez and Dr. Don Ross

Dr. Ramirez

Without a doubt, one of the people who has impacted me the most throughout my ministry in terms of his passion for people and his intention to seek any possible, creative, and original way to share his faith, is my forever friend, Dr. Michael Mills.

In 1993, I met Michael, his wife Denise, and his children Sean and Bryana in Cleveland, Tennessee to interview them as possible teachers and missionaries to the South American Ministerial Seminary that I had reestablished in Quito, Ecuador.

When I looked into Michael's eyes, I observed his passion for Jesus. I immediately understood that Michael and Denise were being appointed by the Holy Spirit as missionaries on a scale that nobody could imagine. Six months after this first meeting, the Mills family had raised their funds to live in Ecuador for one year, and they were ready to learn Spanish and serve the Lord passionately in the ministry.

It would take an entire book to describe the thirty-two years of their ministry in Ecuador, Uruguay, and the many other countries where they have walked, talked, and preached Jesus. They were teachers and church planters. Among many other things, they also created social programs and constructed temples and other spaces to serve children at risk.

In this foreword, I want to rigorously testify that the author of this important volume is not someone who writes merely from research, but a man whose life forcefully and practically represents his passion for the kingdom of God and for people. His ministry has been consistent in modeling transformative, passionate, efficient, and effective discipleship.

In the life of Jesus, it is obvious that "making disciples" was His core goal. I would venture to say that there was no aspect of Jesus' ministry as important as discipleship. Of course, He came to die for our sins and rise from the dead for our justification; but He did all that in a weekend, as far as time is concerned.

In His life, Jesus taught and met with people like Nicodemus and the Samaritan woman, and he resolved huge controversies about being who He claimed to be. But in terms of the time He devoted to the project, and in terms of its crucial importance as a missionary strategy, making disciples was given the primary place in Christ's ministry. He always had time for the people He loved. Sometimes He withdrew "aside" with them to give them His undivided attention. He formed them in His image and likeness and prepared them so that He could leave His work in their hands. Doing this was the heart of His ministry. And I firmly believe that today in our work and in the mission of the church, making disciples demands that same passionate priority.

The twelve disciples were Christ's followers in the strictest sense, His apprentices, His committed "partners" with him in life and death. Later, in the book of Acts, "disciple" is practically synonymous with "Christian" (either we are disciples, or we are not Christians), and some authors, such as Ignatius of Antioch, used the term "disciple" particularly for martyrs.

Another observation: the Synoptic Gospels always speak in the plural of "his disciples," or sometimes "the disciples" (in contrast to John, who almost always uses the singular "disciple," something the Synoptics never do). The concept of being a disciple was a communal one: together, they were "the Twelve." As the ancient people of Israel was founded on the twelve patriarchs and was composed of twelve tribes with their territory and government, so Jesus came to establish his "new people" (the nucleus of the new kingdom) with precisely twelve disciples.

The book of Acts says that Jesus walked everywhere, doing good, and that being a disciple meant walking with Him as He did good, demonstrating the presence and power of the Kingdom of God. Of course, Jesus taught with a lot of authority, and He was very wise, but what distinguished Him from other teachers was His calling of the disciples and the fruit that He produced in them.

Jesus's disciples were called to action in the name of the Lord, with power and authority that no rabbi could share. Discipleship with Jesus was a transformative action. The disciples of Christ learned to be intimately related to Him. He did not tell them, "Follow my doctrine," He simply said, "Follow me." Jesus taught with authority. And from the beginning, He presented himself with a sovereign authority that could only belong to God.

Christian discipleship was and is grace, but not "cheap grace," as Bonhoeffer said. Christ offers everything and demands everything. He tells us, "Freely you received, freely give," and we must give all (Matthew 10:8). Jesus tells us to take up His cross and follow Him with everything we have.

The call that Jesus makes is radical. He appears before a person and commands him to drop everything, commit himself totally and radically to Him, surrender to a totally new lifestyle, and give himself unto death for the cause of the Lord. Jesus leaves no options. His demands are unconditional. From the beginning, Jesus presents Himself as more than just a teacher—He is the Lord of life and death, Lord of all.

Disciples of Jesus never "graduate," they remain lifelong disciples. One is a lifelong disciple, following the Master, until the day of his death. He never stops being an "apprentice" (one who is learning, is training) to become an "authority," an expert. No one graduates from the school of Jesus. Even as "apostles," the Twelve did not cease to be "disciples." They are "those who follow the lamb," according to Revelation. As the ancient theologians said, we are all the "infants" of the Lord.

In over twenty-five years of a ministry relationship with Dr. Michael Mills, I have learned four fundamental truths about discipleship through observing his life and ministry: 1. The disciple "makes room" for the other. Ephesians 2:10 says, "For we are [God's] workmanship, created in Christ Jesus for good works, which God prepared beforehand, that we should walk in them." Disciples help one another to accomplish these good works. 2. Disciples repair weak areas or gaps in the lives of God's people so that they are perfectly qualified to do the work of the ministry (Ephesians 4:16, "so that each part may do its work"). Like the human body, the body of Christ grows through exercise. 3. The disciples are to "equip the saints for the work of the ministry" (Ephesians 4:12). 4. The disciple who forms others decentralizes power, responsibilities, and tasks by equipping and empowering each member of the body of Christ.

Undoubtedly, reading *Arise, Mighty Army: Trinitarian Discipleship* will be a great blessing for the development of personal and community discipleship.

David E. Ramirez, D. Min.
3rd Assistant General Supervisor
Executive Director of Education
Church of God, Cleveland Tennessee

Dr. Ross

I have had the privilege of knowing Dr. Michael Mills for nearly two decades. I have known him both as his pastor and as his denominational overseer. One thing remains strikingly clear: Dr. Mills is completely and radically dedicated to making disciples for Jesus Christ.

Though Jesus gave the command in Matthew 28 to "make disciples," we have largely deviated from that command. In fact, we have chosen to use the word "discipleship" rather than to use the language of our Lord, "make disciples." This is a shift that cannot be overstated, and it must be reconciled with Scripture and the prime directive given to us by our Lord and Savior.

It is entirely possible for someone to be immersed in discipleship in the local church and never completely make a disciple. For us, the term discipleship could be a substitute term for spiritual growth. This means someone could grow spiritually during his or her entire life, always learning something new about following Christ, and never lead anyone to Him. This was not Christ's intention in giving this command.

It is impossible to obey Christ's command to make disciples and never lead someone to Christ. Therefore, making disciples is paramount and rises above the term "discipleship." In fact, it is safe to say that we are not faithful disciples of Jesus if we do not make disciples ourselves.

Consider the fruit of an apple tree. What would you say its fruit is? Some would say an apple and be correct. Others would say that the fruit of an apple tree is the seeds within the apple, and this answer is also correct. But the most complete answer is that the true fruit of an apple tree is another apple tree, because that takes the growth process full cycle.

It is not enough to simply be a disciple of Jesus; we are called to be disciple makers. A disciple maker does not lead someone to Christ and stop there. A true disciple maker will lead someone to Christ and train that person to obey what Jesus taught, baptize them, and then train them to again make another disciple. Simply put, the fruit of a disciple is not another disciple, it is another disciple maker.

This is the complete focus of Dr. Michael Mills's book, *Arise, Mighty Army*. Michael is not declaring that we need to simply lead people to Christ, but that we need to be involved in making disciples who become disciple makers themselves. I could not agree with this more.

In Jesus's teaching, He gave us a job to do, which is to make disciples. By the same token, He told us what His job was: to build the church. In Jesus's radical assignments, we are to make disciples while He builds the church. The challenge in this current time is that we have chosen often to invert those two commands.

By our actions, decisions, and values, we have declared to Christ Himself, "You make disciples, and we will build the church." We have further deceived ourselves into thinking that if we gather a crowd, we are building a church, which is certainly not the truth.

In the most recent pandemic we have survived, one thing has clearly been shown to the church: we must become better at making disciples. Jesus is pruning, sifting, and purging His church to make us the beautiful bride of Christ, without spot or wrinkle. This will only be accomplished through our obedience to His command to "go and make disciples."

The practical approach that Dr. Michael Mills lays out in his book can become a tremendous tool to any Christian leader who chooses to embrace our Lord's command. I am encouraged that you, the reader, are taking this topic of making disciples seriously. If you were not serious about this subject, you would not be reading this book.

I am convinced that when we see Jesus face-to-face, we will not be held responsible for our sin. Jesus has taken care of that on the cross. We will, however, be held responsible for our obedience to Christ while we are here on earth, for how we have lived up to His expectations, obeyed His commands, and reached our full kingdom potential.

I am praying that you will discover the joy of making disciples through your personal obedience.

Sincerely,

Dr. Donald E. Ross,
AG Northwest Ministry Network Leader
and author of *Turnaround Pastor*

Preface

I want to tell you a story...it was the evening of April 14, 1978. This was the precise moment when the Trinity completely captured me. My day started like any other day, but before that evening ended, He had hijacked my entire future.

I was only four months into my twenty-first year of life. I was born in New York, but at seventeen I had joined the Air Force and traveled to Alamogordo, New Mexico. Now that was a life-changing event, and just one of many to come! By that specific day, April 14, I had passed an Air Force exam and faced two future possibilities. The first possibility was a promotion from Buck Sergeant to Second Lieutenant, finally becoming a commissioned officer. The second possibility was to begin flight training as the second person in a jet: a navigator. At just twenty-one years old, I was jazzed!

A week before my eventful night, a new Staff Sergeant, George Lee III, became my supervisor. He had just arrived from being stationed in Spain. During the week, George spouted off some pithy sayings to me. I really did not understand them, but I thought they were cool.

Then, that Thursday, George did something that I believe was illegal evangelism! He invited a single man (me) to have a homecooked meal with him, his wife, and his two children. What is a single guy going to say about a free homecooked meal? Well, let me think about it...YES!

On Friday, April 14, I showed up to eat and meet George's family. I met his wife Sandra and his children George Lee IV and Melissa. We had a delicious home-cooked meal.

Like a disappearing act, everyone but George left to another part of the house. George asked me if I had heard some of the things he had been sharing at work over the last week. When he asked me to share one saying that really stuck with me, I told him, "I remember you said, 'what does it profit a man to gain the whole world, just to lose his soul?'"

As I was raised as a responsible young man, I had developed some atheistic tendencies from my father. Basically, I was spiritually clueless, except for those LONG Jesus letters that my sister Keri faithfully sent to me. Thank you, Keri! You see, I had no clue that I was in God's crosshairs. That night, George was the last of a long line of "spiritual touches" that I had received over the years.

George continued to share the Gospel with me. He asked me if I would like to receive Jesus as my Savior. I said yes, and he asked me to bow my knees and ask Jesus into my heart.

That moment was electrifying for me. It was like I pushed my head through the clouds and saw heaven for the first time in my life. I am crying now, as I write, like I did on that eventful night forty-five years ago. My life was radically changed. I received an unquenchable love for God, a peace that I had never known, a ravenous hunger for His word, and a desire to share what I had received with others.

My love, peace, and joy for God consumed me. Starting the next day, anyone who came within two feet of me needed to hear about what He did for me. George knew that his God had done a wonderful work in Michael Séan Mills. George asked me if I would like him to disciple me for the next year. I responded, "Yes!"

I did not know that his request was not the norm for every new Christian. It turns out that you can bring someone to salvation and leave them to die on the vine. George took a year to disciple me, leading me through the Bible, giving me experiences with God, and showing me how to practically help others to know the Lord—I learned to make disciples. It is no wonder that this book has been boiling in my soul!

I still possess all the zeal of the Spirit that I received in 1978, I just have a lot more wisdom about how to share Jesus with others now. I shared this story because I want you to read *Arise, Mighty Army* to help you obey the command of the Lord. Be personally responsible to create a resurgence of a Jesus movement: make disciples! It is my hope that this book will bring you closer to accomplishing God's task for us in this world.

Chapter One:
T3D International Introduction

Allow me to give you some advice before you read my book. You may feel uncomfortable when you begin reading. One possible reason for this is that the teaching in the book disassembles how we learned to make disciples in the past. The book then rebuilds a Trinitarian understanding of biblical discipleship training. My book challenges you to have a heartfelt understanding of what it means to have an intimate relationship with the Trinity. You may not see God as our relational God, but that is who He is.

Also, there are a lot of new and difficult theological terms in my book. Do not be afraid. As you continue to read and learn, I will simplify the terms. You may want to read over the material a few times to let it soak in. Do not get stuck in one place. Keep reading! The best way to understand my book is to select others to study with you and absorb the book as a team—or, if you will, as disciples.

If you use this book with others, you can converse about each chapter in a devotional style. You might find yourself actively making a disciple exactly as the Lord commanded. If you get stuck, ask the author! You can contact me at: "_T3DInternationalDisciples4Him@ gmail.com._" I love helping others to obey the Lord's command to make disciples.

I want to add that I will use the concept Trinity interchangeably with the individual names of the Godhead, each of them divine and equal. This way you will know that when I refer to the Father, Son, or Holy Spirit, I refer to their unity as one, the personhood of the triune God.

Who Should Be Trained with T3D International?

The teaching that I began is called "T3D." The meaning of this acronym will be fully explained in Chapter Two. Who should be personally trained to be a T3D disciple? My discipleship program is based on the

Bible; everyone is welcome to learn how to make a disciple. I believe that people in a younger age range may not understand the concept of making disciples. I also believe that people in an upper age range may not be able to manage the full workload that is needed to make disciples. However, I maintain that the Lord oversees all age ranges. Jehoash was only seven years old when he became king of Judah in the Old Testament. You are reading this book. That is proof that God has need of you to apply its teaching to others.

I believe that many Christians around the world have learned that making a disciple is important. However, I do not think they know how to make one. They understand the concept of making disciples, but because they do not know how to accomplish the task practically, they do not.

Over the last few years, I have trained over 1,200 disciples as T3D leaders in four different countries: the United States, Uruguay, Ecuador, and Kenya. These disciples range from age thirteen to ninety-five, from wealthy to impoverished, and from the educated to those who only graduated the sixth grade. Some felt like the Lord no longer wanted to use them, because they were not educated or wealthy; these became some of my best disciple makers!

Applying the teaching of my book results in two incredible outcomes: people get excited about learning how to make disciples, and they systematically begin to train disciples with the information that they learned. If you teach others how to make disciples using the principles of this book, they will in turn teach others. That is what Jesus did.

Where and Why Should You Make Disciples?

Why should you make disciples? You are a direct descendant of Jesus's disciples. Where would you be if the original twelve decided not to make disciples? For me, the overwhelming response to "why" is because Jesus asked you to make disciples. T3D was a program that was given to me for the entire world to use. Let us consider the antithesis of this idea. What would happen if you do not continue to make disciples? Who will no longer be a disciple in the future if you opt out now?

Where can you make disciples? Everywhere, wherever you are! The location does not matter, it is only important that we are always systematically making disciples. I use a narrow meaning of the word discipleship: the process of making others who follow Jesus as they become more doctrinally Christ-like. Make sure you have someone training up disciples working with you as you train disciples.

Always train disciples like Jesus did, "in your going." This is the definition of the passive Greek verb for "go" found in Matthew 28:19. As Jesus did with His disciples, you can also learn to live life with your disciples. Spend time with them, pointing out life lessons while making scriptural connections. This book gives you the structure to purposefully share your life with and teach others. Training a disciple means sharing life with them through the good times, tough times, happy times, sad times, successful times, and non-successful times.

I spent nine of my twenty-two years in Ecuador as a pastor. At one of my pastoral leadership meetings, I asked my associate pastors one by one what would happen to their ministry if they died today. They all stated that their ministry would stop. I asked them, "What if I died today?" They responded, "Sorry to tell you, pastor, but your ministry would keep going, because you have formed us as disciples." I said, "Do not be sorry, you are responding correctly." Leaders should be training leaders to replace themselves. Leadership is not lonely if you are constantly training others.

Why Should You Train to Be a T3D Disciple?

Disciple making is accomplished by those with a voluntary heart. Training disciples is not a paid gig. The Lord's army is made up of volunteers. If you want to work in His army, it will require a lot of work and a voluntary heart. Brigadier General James Doolittle once said, "Nothing is as strong as the heart of a volunteer"[1] He said this as he was asking eighty trained soldiers and pilots to fly a very dangerous mission during World War II. The men were likely to lose their lives,

---

[1] Jeff Thatcher, "Nothing Stronger," Arkansas Online, July 22, 2023, https://www.arkansasonline.com/news/2021/sep/16/nothing-stronger/.

but all eighty men stepped forward to volunteer. I am asking you to volunteer to complete this program and train at least one disciple.

I have written this book so each new generation of T3D disciples will maintain theological integrity. If the book was not written, future leaders would not be able to maintain the structure and theological integrity of the program. Since the T3D curriculum uses teaching from the Bible, future generations can follow the same teaching without losing any important information.

T3D is a structured program that you can learn from. Then your disciples can use this material, and so can their disciples. You need to train as a T3D disciple so God can bless you as you obey His word. You must be a disciple before you can train other disciples.

I have primarily taught this program in the United States and South and Central America. I have learned that many Christians in many nations no longer systematically train disciples to obey the Word of God. My heart is broken, and I want to make a difference in God's kingdom. I am going to start with you. It is my grand experiment.

If you get excited about the training program contained in this book, together we can start a world revolution of making disciples. Our goal is to start a worldwide resurgence of Jesus's movement to systematically make disciples.

The Origin of T3D International

This book stems from my doctoral writings while I was completing my Doctor of Ministries degree at Asbury Theological Seminary. I attended Asbury with a Beeson scholarship, as part of a program funded by a bequest from Ralph Beeson. Beeson wanted to see Asbury train leaders from around the world and help visionary pastors continue their education.

Halfway through my studies, I was prompted by the Holy Spirit to momentarily lay aside my doctoral work. Over the course of a few hours, I wrote down everything that He prompted in my heart. This was the core to the T3D International program of Trinitarian Discipleship.

Chapter Two:
T3D Operating System

In this chapter, I want to explain each component of the book's title.

Arise

The title starts with the word "arise." I used the word "arise" because I believe that many well-meaning disciples of Christ are sitting in the pews of churches rather than "going" into the harvest field, winning souls, and training disciples.

When Saul was on his way to kill those who invoked the name of Christ, he encountered the Lord. The Lord knocked him to the ground, spoke to him, and led him away "blind." Saul needed to "arise" from the ground. The Lord wanted to use Saul to make disciples and leaders, much like He wants to use you. We need to reread this account today with eyes on the harvest of untrained disciples.

At the precise moment of his encounter, Saul was "set on foot." Saul, a man of many eloquent words, was rendered "speechless." He had to be "led by hand." During the time he was blinded, the powerful Word of Jesus burned in his heart, and then the Holy Spirit guided him.[2]

The Holy Spirit equipped Saul and gave him the name of Paul. Paul had a new vision to make disciples, baptizing them in the name of Jesus, actively obeying Christ's mandate. Many Christians today are not obeying the Great Commission. What would have happened if Jesus's disciples had decided not to make disciples? Where would you be today? The word of the Lord is Matthew 28:19, "...go and make disciples..." baptizing them in the Trinity.

From God's perspective, "go" means that you are in one place with your own understanding of who He is, and God wants you in another place with a Trinitarian understanding of who He is. Trinitarian

---

[2] H. D. M. Spence-Jones, ed., The Pulpit Commentary: The Acts of the Apostles, vol. 1 (London; New York: Funk & Wagnalls Company, 1909).

doctrine is based on understanding the social and relational aspects of the triune God. Christians would like to train disciples, but they do not know how. They need time to hear His word, be led by the hand through a time of instruction (precisely the training T3D offers), and receive sight and new vision from the Trinity.

Mighty Army

Why is "Mighty Army" part of the book title? During my forty-five years of experience in Christ, it has been my belief that the incredible army of the Lord is in repose! The army is not obeying Jesus's command to "make disciples." When we get back to making disciples like He commanded, a mighty army of His disciples will form across the globe.

I have trained over 1,200 T3D leaders. To understand where each of them were in the art of making disciples, I asked them three questions at the beginning of their training. First, I asked Question One: Do you believe as a Christian that it is important to make disciples? They all responded with a hearty "Yes!" Then I asked Question Two: Does the Bible teach that it is important to make disciples? Again, they said "Yes!" I also asked a Question Two-and-a-Half: What verse in the Bible states that we should make disciples? The majority confessed they did not know where the verse was located, but that they knew it could be found somewhere in the Bible. I told them it was not their fault they did not know where the scripture was; it was my fault as a leader for not specifically teaching them where the Bible verse was located.

After I restated their answers—that they believed making disciples was important, and that the Bible stated it was important to make disciples—I asked Question Three: How many of you have systematically trained anyone to be a disciple for Christ in the past year? The answer was none of them.

You cannot be a Mighty Army if you do not obey your commander's command. Pastors and church leaders have successfully convinced young Christians that they must train other Christians—that they must make disciples. Although as leaders we have successfully made this work important, I believe that we have never trained Christians "how" to make a disciple. T3D International teaches every believer how to obey God's Word and make a disciple.

Permit me to do a quick evaluation of you. I want to ask you the same personal question. How many disciples have you systematically trained to be like Christ during this last year? Out of over 1,200 people I have asked in five different countries, nobody has reported to me that he or she has systematically made a single disciple. There is a mighty army ready to be deployed into God's service, but the army is seated. Although the members of this army have been in ready mode for a long time, they have not yet engaged in His service. The power of the Holy Spirit was never meant for those who remain seated. The Spirit will empower and infill us as we get up and go into our world for His sake.

Our world of influence, according to Acts 1:8, is local; further away; and from our home to the nations and the entire globe. Where is the Holy Spirit leading you? Go and make disciples! It is impossible for you to "go" and remain where you are! The word "go" is passively used in Matthew 28:19. In this verse, the word "go" means "in your going." While you live out your Christian life in Jesus, share Him with others. Engage others and be kind to them as you are going. Your hope is to win some with your lifestyle. God may not ask you to "go" to other lands, but He has asked you to share your life with others, working where you are now.

You must also train others who are currently within your reach. Jesus's command is "make disciples." This command to make disciples is different than the command to "go." The discipleship command has a longer timeframe, involves a group of people, and requires more intention. This command is something we are not systematically doing. God will personally lead us while we are speechless and blind. He will lead us towards His vision, "go and make disciples." I am convinced that if the mighty army of God rises and asks for the infilling of the Holy Spirit, specifically for the purpose of training other disciples, then the Lord will empower His army to transform this world. He will help the army of disciples to train and equip others. You will be obeying His word in Matthew 28:19, and He will rejoice and bless your obedience!

Trinitarian Discipleship

Why is Trinitarian Discipleship in the title? The creation of the concept of Trinity is attributed to the early church father Tertullian. Early Christians tried to grasp the meaning of a "three in one Godhead." Biblical commentator Paul Molnar suggests that the Trinity needs to be perceived through an understanding of a social and relational Godhead.[3] His words move us toward trusting that our God is relational. I purpose that the Trinity wants an intimate relationship with the creation. The word "Trinity" is not found in the Bible. However, the formula of Father, Son, and Holy Spirit is found throughout the Bible. You would be surprised at the number of times the formula appears in the Bible.

As we learn about discipleship, we will need to understand how the Trinity wants a resurgent movement based on what Jesus began. This movement is active, vibrant, and alive now. T3D International is a global movement that will spontaneously revitalize the sleeping church.

We must remember that the Holy Spirit is the third person of the Trinity. The personal infilling and empowering of the Holy Spirit are important to all who want to obey His commands. The Holy Spirit is a constant throughout the Old and New Testaments. If we ask, He will grant us access to the full power of the Trinity so we can enact the commands of God in this world.

During the celebration of Pentecost in the New Testament, Christ's disciples received the baptism of the Holy Spirit. Acts 1:8 and 2:4 recount the Holy Spirit's infilling of the followers of Christ during this celebration. These are two important scriptures for Christians filled with the Holy Spirit. Acts 1:8 tells believers that they will receive power after the Holy Spirit comes upon them.

The word "power" in this verse is the word "dunamus" in the original language. This is the base word from which we get the English term

---

[3] Paul D. Molnar, "The Trinity and the Freedom of God," Journal for Christian Theological Research 8 (2003), https://digitalcommons.luthersem.edu/jctr/vol8/iss2003/1/.

"dynamite." Dynamite is an explosive power. As we ask for His power in our lives, God's world-changing power will explode inside us. There is a marked difference in Jesus's twelve disciples before and after the baptism of the Holy Spirit. Look at Peter's life—he experienced a powerful Holy Spirit change between the time he denied Christ publicly and the day he began to preach in the book of Acts.

Acts 1:8 tells the receivers of the Holy Spirit that they will be "witnesses." We are to be witnesses of Christ in our personal worlds: local, neighborhoods, state, nation and to the uttermost parts of the earth. Although many believers today view Acts 1:8 as a mandate from God of being filled by Him, they do not know the meaning of this scripture.

In the original language, the word "witnesses" means "martyr." Acts 1:8 describes those receiving power when the Holy Spirit comes on them as becoming His martyrs. A martyr is someone who gives the ultimate gift of self-sacrifice. A Christian asks God to be filled by the Holy Spirit, to be a martyr, so a lost world can know the living savior. The power of the Holy Spirit is not to be consumed by the individuals who receive it. Yes, the Holy Spirit will guide, heal, and protect us, but when we ask Him into our lives, He pushes us out of our comfort zones to minister to those who need the love of the Trinity. We are to go with Him to reach the lost and make disciples.

For my dissertation research, I wanted to see if I could convince two groups of fifty people to use their own ideas and money to minister to people fifty miles away. One group was from San Cristóbal Island in the Galápagos, and the other was from the mainland of Ecuador. My two research groups all declared that they were filled with the Holy Spirit. As I evaluated my research data, my serendipitous finding was that both groups had consumed the power of the Holy Spirit. They declared that the Holy Spirit had guided them, healed them, and used them for His work. His power seemed to be concentrated within them.

According to Acts 1:8 and 2:4, the Lord does not just minister to our hearts, but also pushes us to go outside into a lost world with His "dunamus" Holy Spirit power. Remember, the word "dunamus" is the root word for dynamite. If you are handed a lit piece of dynamite, you will throw it as far away as you can so it does not explode near you. Reading Acts 1:8 with your heart means that you are asking the Holy Spirit's power to come into your life. He will explode from the inside out in your life!

Never smother the Holy Spirit. The purpose of His infilling power has never been to sit within the four walls of the church. The Holy Spirit filled the early church, and its members sat with His explosive power until in Acts 8:1 it became clear that Christians living in the Roman empire would experience constant persecution. At this point in church history, the believers filled with the Holy Spirit arose and began to "go." Acts 8:1 propelled the receivers of God's Word to obey Acts 1:8, to go to the uttermost parts of the world. Acts 1:8 mentioned that once the believers were filled with the Holy Spirt, they were to go out into their local areas and then go further out until they reached the uttermost parts of the world. Yet they did not leave Jerusalem until Acts 8:1. It was then that God gave them persecution and they left Jerusalem to reach the world.

Is God making us uncomfortable where we are so we can engage the power of the Holy Spirit from inside our hearts to go to those who are outside and need Him around the world? We need to be witnesses of the mighty God. Highlighting Him as the only God in our lives demonstrates that we do not live in a world of many gods. This distinction was mightily witnessed in the redemption of God's people from Egypt. Egypt had a god for everything. The Hebrew God was one God.

T3D International

What does T3D International signify? If you are using this book to train others, you need to ensure that your students know the meaning of T3D International. This is a core part of what you will teach others. Make sure that you and your students can easily explain what T3D signifies.

When the Holy Spirit asked me to put aside my doctoral work, He wanted to share a strategy for T3D International, a Trinitarian discipleship program. Over a few hours as the Holy Spirit dictated to me, I transcribed the outline for what I now call the T3D International program. The symbols of T3D International hold the following meanings: T = Trinity. 3 = 3 in One; Father, Son, and Holy Spirit. D = three disciples trained every three months. These concise symbols were expanded into a once a week, three-month training program for the interior of Uruguay.

At the time of the writing of this book, I am scheduled to teach this program in Slovakia, England, Scotland, Ireland, and possibly in Wales. I am aware that the Trinity wants to use the T3D International program in different countries, for the entire Christian population.

The Lion in Repose

The cover of the book depicts a majestic lion in a reposed position. A lion demonstrates its power when it is active. Even the enemy is described in the Bible as being "like a roaring lion" (1 Peter 5:8b). The enemy is "like" a roaring lion. I do not want the church to be "like" a mighty army, I want the church to *be* a mighty army, a powerful and active lion. The army of God must engage this world now; be mighty! Psalm 68:11 says, "The Lord gives the word, and a great army brings the good news" (NLT). We must be that army.

My son Sean shared that he believes the lion on the cover is a bit of a plot twist. You think at first this must be the Lion of Judah, but you must get to the end of the book and see through new eyes. When you study the book, you discover that the church "should" be the Lion of Judah. However, around the world, many of you "lions of God" are sound asleep. We all must arise, shake ourselves, be active, and obey Jesus's command: make disciples!

Chapter Three:
Pre-T3D International

Before we begin the T3D International training, I want to share what I call pre-T3D. You need to share pre-T3D with anyone you select to study with you. In the beginning of your study, I ask you to pray about reading this book. If you study this book as a devotional, consider people who might study with you and ask them to pray before deciding to join you.

This step of prayer is necessary to give your disciples several days to ask God if He wants them to study this program. It is important to personally know that it is His will for you to complete the work of this book. You will learn in the next chapters of this book that the Trinity is going to break down some of your old and not-so-useful epistemologies. The Trinity will then build you back up with new and valuable knowledge of how to make disciples.

I will explain a few simple and successful requirements for you to complete the T3D International program. I use the word "requirement" because we all need a gentle nudge to complete any new and challenging process in our lives. Although these requirements are simple to read, they will require work. The Trinity requires us to obey what is biblically asked of us. We cannot stay where we are spiritually, mentally, or physically and obey His word to "go." Training requires work if we are to be successful.

There are five requirements for completing the T3D International program.

1. Choose Your Disciples

Write down your own name and the names of the three disciples you will train. Do this step right away during the first few weeks of training. Everyone who is trained by reading this book must write their own name and the names of three disciples who will participate with them on a piece of paper, cardboard, or on a computer. These names should be in a place where they can be seen and prayed for each day. You need something visible to remind you to pray daily for your future disciples. Each of your trainees will do the same, writing their names on a piece of paper and leaving three lines to insert the names of future disciples.

I want you to choose three disciples in the beginning. Never count anyone out. Believe that God wants to train them to be disciples! As quickly as possible (in the next few weeks), choose a minimum of three disciples who you will teach. Write their names down in a prominent place. If you do not take this step right away, you will not plan to make a disciple.

This is a pivotal step. As you begin to pray for your three candidates, you will sense a special touch from the Trinity. The Trinity is there to quell any fear that may arise. Do not worry. You will be using this book as you teach your team of disciples. You will not be doing anything different than what you are doing now as you study. The Lord is very pleased with you for making even one disciple. Remember, if you can train one, you can train two.

Tell the people whose names you have written down that you are learning how to make disciples and that you have chosen them to study with you. Pick a comfortable time and place to go through this book as a team. You can tell them that you are willing to do a group devotional, train a larger group, or train them individually, always using this book as a guide. If, for any reason, one of your chosen disciples does not want to study with you, replace their name with another. Do not worry about missing them now, it is more than likely that they will join you at a future time. Some people like to see if you will be successful before they join in.

2. Set a Schedule and Timeline for Your Study

Remember, you do not need to complete the study in the same twelve-week timeline that I use. You can complete the book in a shorter or longer period. I used a three-month timeline because I was teaching more than three people. I was teaching 200 people at a time, both in Ecuador and in Uruguay, so I needed specific days and times to teach. My goal was to graduate large groups of new disciples so that they could begin training others, who would in turn train others. The study rate for you and your disciples will depend on how quickly you understand the material and how soon you are ready to make another disciple. Start by making one disciple, then work your way up to training three at a time.

You do not need to be concerned about the time of day and day of the week to train. You may find that 5 a.m. on a Monday or 7 p.m. on a Thursday is the best time to train. You are free to select what is best for you.

If you need more time to go through the material presented, take as much time as you need. Teach at a comfortable speed for you and your disciples. Training disciples is the most important thing; it does not matter how quickly you train them! The goal of this book is to help you obey God's command in Matthew 28:19.

Even if some of the people you are training begin and leave the program after several weeks, keep inviting them back until the course has finished. They may want to begin again. The fact is that you are committed to obeying God's Word to make disciples. Keep praying for them. Keep inviting them to learn how to be disciples and make disciples.

It is critical that you do not skip any of the teaching chapters in this book. I authored this book so I could support the theological integrity of T3D International. Right now, there are some churches in Uruguay and Ecuador who have taught T3D International for three different generations. When I say generations, I mean that I taught the material the first time, and now, without my direct intervention, they have used my material to teach three disciples each, during three consecutive months. They have used this material to teach teenagers, young adults, married couples, and older adults. Teach T3D International to anyone who will obey what Jesus commanded. Make disciples!

My immediate concern is whether each generation is teaching the theology of T3D International correctly. There is a game called "telephone," where a person whispers a phrase in someone's ear. This person in turn whispers the phrase in someone else's ear, until many people have heard the phrase. The problem is that the end phrase is nothing like the initial phrase. The purpose of T3D International is for everyone around the world to teach and begin making disciples. With my book I can more easily ensure the theological integrity of the program.

I understand that your free will is involved when God asks you to do something. So please pause now for a season of prayer. Seriously ask God if He wants you to complete the T3D International program. If He says no, take a step back and re-engage at another time. If He says yes, then do what you need to do to complete all the work that is required. It is important to me that I tell you ahead of time about the work and commitment that is involved in making disciples. I want you to engage your will and determination to finish this training and begin teaching three others. Give all the disciples you will train this same chance to take time to pray. My hope is that you all will continue.

It is important that each person is aware of the work that needs to be done over the next weeks. I am not going to lie to you, there is work to be done. I believe that you can do the work as you pray for God's strength. It is true that you are praying to see if the Lord wants you to complete this study. But the absolute truth is that God has already asked you to go on this journey with Him. He has great plans for you and the future leaders you will touch for His glory. The Trinity is very interested in you obeying His command in Matthew 28:19.

If you begin reading the book, others can read with you as you go through the material. Each time a group completes the study, they need to rest for a few days and then begin teaching the same material to at least three more disciples. When your disciples go through the material with you, it will be easier for them to follow your example and train their disciples.

After a time of prayer asking God if He wants you to study T3D International, start with the following basic teaching. Welcome everyone who is studying with you. Remember that in these next weeks or months, you want to get as close as you can with your new disciples, just as Christ did as He led his disciples during His three years of ministry. He walked from town to town with them, taught them "as they were going," and spent His time with them. Take time to know your disciples and share who you are. When I taught in Ecuador, my disciples were surprised to learn that my dad was born in Glasgow, Scotland. Share life together; Jesus did. This may be difficult if you train others over a distance. Be creative. Find a way to learn more about your disciples as you share who you are.

3. Get a One Year Bible and Read Every Day

Get a One Year Bible and keep reading this book. The One Year Bible consists of the Old Testament, New Testament, Proverbs, and Psalms divided over 365 days. I only suggest a One Year Bible because that is what I use, but you can use any Bible of your choosing. I am asking you to use a One Year Bible format so you can get into a habit of reading the Bible. Plus, I would love to be reading the same verses as you on the same day. Many people have reported to me the hundreds of Bible versions or apps versions they have. When I ask how many times they have systematically read the Bible, there is a notable silence. I want to create a disciple making culture that involves reading God's Word daily.

The daily reading of the Bible is central to the T3D International study. At least make a commitment to read God's Word over the days it takes you to read my book. I believe that the only way that you, a Gentile, will have a deep consciousness of God's character and identity is if you read His Word daily. The Jewish people have learned about God experientially for thousands of years. They instruct their children about who God is each day through a teaching called the Shema. What do the Gentiles teach their children? Where to cross the street?

Try to read God's Word at each day for at least three months using any Bible. You can use a One Year Bible, or purchase any Bible and download a free one-year guide online. You can even read the Bible for free on Google or listen to an audiobook version of the Bible each day. The important thing is that you make a habit of interacting with His Word each day. The point I care about most is that Christians are reading their Bibles and communicating with God daily. You must be His disciple before you can train other disciples.

When you are using my book to teach a team, allow your students to share something each time you meet to cover a chapter. This can be something that God used to touch their hearts from my book or from the Bible. Discuss the book chapter with the team openly. Consider assigning one disciple per class to share for five minutes about the reading that week. When people "share," the goal is not for them to reread what they read during the week, but to explain from their hearts how God personally used what they highlighted.

Since the disciples are assigned to read the One Year Bible each day, a second student can share for five minutes about a Bible passage in the same way, describing something relational that the Trinity used to touch his or her heart. When God touches someone's heart, He is speaking to the disciple about what they are reading in the Bible or the book. God is the God of "dirty Bibles." He does not want us to get to heaven with important books and Bibles that have never been worked through daily. He would rather these items be stained with years of rumpled pages, notes, tears, and highlights.

My hope is that daily Bible reading will become a habit for the rest of your life. Whatever Bible you choose, read enough to complete the Bible in one year. That is the goal. At the time of the writing of this book, I have read my Bible forty-seven times from Genesis to Revelation. I believe in what I am asking you to do.

4. Complete the Chapter Workbooks

You must fill out the blanks after each chapter. There will be a section marked "T3D International Workbook." All students should fill in the blanks in the workbook at the end of each chapter to complete the course. The answer for most blanks can be found in the chapter that you just finished reading. A few blanks will require you to think and respond. In these cases, there are no wrong answers, just thoughtful ones. You can do it!

My goal in having you fill out the blanks after each chapter is to allow the material to simmer into your heart and mind. The more times you interact with the material, the better you will absorb the idea of making a disciple. In the following chapters, you will be given biblical information about how the Trinity wants you to make a disciple.

5. Complete a Social/Evangelistic Project

All T3D International disciples must complete a Social/Evangelistic Project. More information about this can be found in Chapter Twelve. This section is just an outline of the work that you are required to do as a disciple of T3D International; Chapter Twelve will give you all the details needed to complete your project. About halfway through the teaching chapters, you and your team should begin working on your Social/Evangelistic Project.

The Social/Evangelistic Project is the core teaching through which you will learn about giving to others. Through this project, you will allow the Holy Spirit to use you to bless someone else. The theological teachings I will share with you will illustrate how an unselfish Jesus gave to others in need. He taught His disciples how to make disciples with a heart full of His love. There is no way to teach this information unless you complete a Social/Evangelistic Project.

When you and your team plan your Social/Evangelistic Project, you must plan it in such a way that the people you help will ask the following question: Who is your God, and why are you doing this for me? Examples of these projects and their outcomes are given in Chapter Twelve.

Let us begin. From this point on, what you read and learn in my book is what you will teach your personal disciples. This book is to be put into practice. Highlight the important concepts that you read and teach those concepts to your disciples. If you are studying this book with a group as a devotional, have everyone read the chapters before you meet to discuss the book together. Study my book by sipping on the chapters; do not gulp them.

The teaching continues in the next ten chapters, which are the core of the T3D International theology. It is very important to teach all your students to study these next chapters as closely as possible. Do not stray; ensure that each disciple knows the material presented in my book. Have the students highlight portions of the book and ask questions for open discussion.

Do not get scared as you read and teach this book to your new disciples. Some will understand what is written right away and some will learn on the way. Read the chapters twice before you teach others. If you dare to instruct a small group of leaders (five or more), you will become the best teacher ever. You will become a wonderful instructor and learn more as you teach your first group by faith.

Trust the Holy Spirit to inspire you. The goal at first is not for you to understand everything you read, but for you to begin making disciples and learning together with them. Make sure that all your disciples have this book to study from as you teach. Learn the deep riches of what is written. My two overarching goals in authoring this book are that will you enter an intimate relationship with God, and that you get excited about doing His will to go and make disciples.

This book is a structured way to teach others what the scriptures say about making a disciple. It is presented in a way that will guide you to make disciples, who make disciples, who make other disciples. If everyone makes three disciples each time they read the book, we will start the resurgence of Christ's discipleship movement, as He did when He discipled His original Twelve. Let's make disciples! The Trinity is thrilled about your obedience and will bless you in a very specific way!

Chapter Four:
Epistemology and the Theology of the Great Commission

In this chapter I want to give you a new T3D International greeting that I created, then briefly define two new terms, and finally help you understand a theology of discipleship.

First, I will teach you a new T3D International greeting. I want you to make sure that everyone you teach understands this new greeting, which is called "I Am an Original." For this greeting, make a fist with your left hand with your palm facing upward (switch hands if you are left-handed). Extend your left index finger, then sweep your right index finger across your left index finger from the base of your finger to the tip. End the movement by holding up your right index finger so everyone can see your fingerprints and declare, "I am an original!" The disciple you greet should respond in kind.

Teach your disciples the importance of being an original. If you bought a Picasso painting, it would cost millions of dollars. Why? Because if it is an original, it will cost more to buy. Consider what you are worth. Though this is not an official theology, I believe that when God formed you in your mother's womb (Jeremiah 1:5), He signed you as one of a kind, an original, by giving you unique fingerprints!

My daughter (Bryana) did some medical studies, and she shared some facts with me about the gestation process. When a baby is immersed in amniotic fluid, the fingertips and toe prints are softer than the rest of the skin. You can check the truth of this even now. If you are in water for a certain amount of time, the skin on your digits will shrivel up like a prune. Bryana told me that when a baby is in amniotic fluid for nine months, there is a lot of movement. The fluid washes over each digit and forms the prints. Every baby moves differently. If you want to blow your mind with the great creativity and intelligence of God, research loops, whorls, and arches!

God is omniscient and forms each new creation without duplicating what He has done before or what He will form in the future. He designed enough combinations of loops, whorls, and ridges for an infinite number of individuals to be signed by Him! Your ten fingertips and ten toe pads were designed by God.

Also, think about how God designed your DNA with your own personal characteristics. But not even identical twins, who have the same DNA, will have the same fingerprint. Of all the people who have lived, are alive now, and will be born, no two people have the same friction ridges and recesses on ten fingers and ten toes! One fingerprint is enough for you to say that you are an original and that God loves you. Just as a collector pays more for an original piece of art than for a copy, God also pays the maximum amount for an original. He bought your soul with His Son's own blood! "I Am an Original!"

Now I want to teach you two essential terms: epistemology and theology. Do not worry about how cerebral the words appear. I will help you understand the meaning of every difficult word in this book.

The first word is "epistemology." This word is weighty. In Chapter Ten, I will give you a free word that cost me sixty thousand dollars during my doctoral studies. For now, let me help you understand how epistemology will be used for the T3D International discipleship training course.

The word epistemology will be explained more fully when the "Theology of Two Epistemologies: Gnosis and Yada" is taught in the next chapter. For now, you need to understand that epistemology is the science of how we learn or know what we know at the present time. As a child, you may have learned that putting your finger into a wall outlet will shock you. Most children only need to learn this lesson once in their entire life. If we apply the science of epistemology, we can say that the child learned through experience.

The second word that is important to us is "theology." "Theology" is a combination of two Greek words: *theos*, which signifies "God" (who we find in the Old and New Testaments), and *logos*, which signifies "rational thought and the word." Simply defined, theology is the study of God. This definition of the "study of God" will include the Trinity.

In this book, we will study God by considering His intimate relationship with us. I want to point out specific scriptures that show the Trinity's self-revelation and how it impacts our human experience. Of course, when we study the Word to study God, it is considered biblical theology. Remember that as we study Him, He is studying us. What you are studying now is considered a part of systematic theology. In systematic theology, Christian doctrines and faith interact with reason, culture, and the natural sciences. We will study God as we see Him through the lenses of the Bible and these concepts.

In this book, you will learn key biblical theologies pertaining to T3D International discipleship. Each theology will explain a study about God and who He is in relation to training disciples. As you teach the theologies of this book to your disciples, the Holy Spirit and His Word will permeate your spirit.

In the next chapter, I will explain the word "epistemology" further. I will also tie two epistemologies together, Gnosis and Yada. I will show how we may have learned discipleship in the past and explain why these two epistemologies need to be married together. Do not let the words "Gnosis" and "Yada" scare you. For now, the meaning of "Gnosis" is "mind," and "Yada" is "heart." These two words are explained in the next chapter.

For the rest of the chapter, I want to teach you how the theology of discipleship is a study of God. The theology of discipleship is a study of God because the Trinity ordained discipleship. This book will concentrate on the importance of discipleship from Jesus's perspective.

Jesus gave His life to free the world from the slavery of sin. After Jesus's resurrection, His first concern was the Great Commission. The first command He gave to His disciples was "go and make disciples." Jesus knew that making disciples was a mission that would show humans their true value and purpose in the world and allow them to develop a greater understanding of who God is. The Trinity has showed love since before the beginning of time, and Jesus continues to promise His love to those who obey His commands. In Exodus 20:6, God says that He "show[s] love to a thousand generations of those who love me and keep my commandment."

You are obeying Jesus's command by making disciples. I want to create a movement that will effectively show His love for another thousand generations. Using the theologies in my book, I will demonstrate "how" to make disciples. You can use the same theologies to help others to train in the same way.

This next thought will blow your mind. Preacher Robert Schuller once said, "Any[one] can count the seeds in an apple, but only God can count the apples in one seed!"[4] In the Great Commission, the disciples were apples in a seed. You are an apple in a seed as well. As you teach others to be disciples, you will be a part of adding future apples to a seed. Think about it—you are a direct disciple of the original Twelve. If you use this book to train other disciples, who train other disciples, who train other disciples...well, you get it! However, this thought becomes negative if you choose not to make disciples. That is why God chose you and wants you to be a disciple who trains other disciples.

In my book, you will learn that God is at work around you, that He believes in you, and that He is choosing you right now to work with Him to learn how to be a disciple and train three new disciples (who train others to be disciples). To be disciples and train others, we must be students of His word. Let me explain a chapter in Matthew using a Yada (heart) approach rather than a Gnosis (mind) approach. Now we will delve into a deep study of the theology of discipleship.

Before we study Matthew 28:16-20, we need to appreciate what transpired at the beginning of the chapter. In the beginning of Matthew 28, the angel dramatically came down to the tomb, rolled away the stone, and sat there. Here we see a display of Trinity power like Jesus used in John 18 when all who were against Him fell like dead men (as you will read in Chapter Eleven). When the tomb guards saw what the angel did, and that Jesus had been resurrected from the grave, they fainted like dead men (Matthew 28:4). In verse seven, then angel told

---

[4] Robert Schuller, Facebook, September 19, 2011, https://www.facebook.com/254517043904/posts/any-fool-can-count-the-seeds-in-an-apple-but-only-god-can-count-the-apples-in-on/10150338747923905/.

the women to have the disciples meet Jesus in Galilee. In verse 10, Jesus Himself gave the women this message.

Matthew 28:16-20 is a core scripture for T3D International. This scripture is commonly referred to as the "Great Commission." Many do not include Matthew 28:16, "Then the eleven disciples went to Galilee, to the mountain where Jesus had told them to go," in the Commission. I want to include this verse, as well as Mark 14:28: "But after I have risen, I will go ahead of you into Galilee." In Matthew, Jesus asked the disciples to go ahead of Him to Galilee. The scripture from Mark talks about where Jesus would go after His resurrection… Galilee! This is exactly where he told His eleven disciples to go. Does that seem strange to you?

After the great display of power from the Trinity, Jesus urgently asked His eleven disciples to go and meet Him in Galilee. Whenever God says "go," He means that you are in one place, and He wants you to come to the place He wants. He wants us to constantly be in a place to obey Him. This "go" is for sure connected to Matthew 28:19, which says "go and make disciples."

I also want to connect God's command to "go" with our early epistemologies. We may not have learned to obey His commands as children. We need to relearn how to "go." Our childhood experiences (from when we did not have the ability to judge the truth) may not be enough for us to obey the Great Commission. Now, as adults, we are informed with biblical and practical experiences of who God is. We now have the ability to judge correctly. We are the ones who need to move when He says "go." "Go" does not always signify an overseas assignment (it can), but it certainly signifies moving from where you are—even if it is just moving across the street to talk to someone different than you. The meaning of "go" could be finishing this book and training other disciples around the world with T3D International.

In today's theology, we will study Mathew 28:16, 18 and 19 from the perspective of Yada (heart-knowledge).

Matthew 28:16 says that Jesus told the "eleven" to meet Him. One was missing. Who? I will not tell you right away. I want you to think about who was missing. Jesus asked eleven disciples to meet Him; I thought that there were twelve disciples.

You will quickly apprehend that Judas is missing. He is one disciple who decided not to do the Great Commission. Peter explained to the new church what had happened to Judas in Acts 1:15-20. I do not believe that Judas was predestined to die in sin; satan deceived him and he yielded to evil. Jesus came to rescue every living soul, even Judas. Jesus washed his feet. How can you not repent with Jesus kneeling in front of you, looking into your eyes while washing your feet? It was Jesus's way of saying to Judas, "I still love you; you are one of mine."

I can say that Jesus washed Judas feet, because of the evidence that we read in John chapter 13. We can see that He washed Judas's feet before the Passover. John writes, "It was just before the Passover Festival….so [Jesus] got up from the meal, took off his outer clothing, and wrapped a towel around his waist. After that, he poured water into a basin and began to wash his disciples' feet….After He had said this, Jesus was troubled in spirit and testified, 'Very truly I tell you, one of you is going to betray me.'" (John 13:1, 4-5, 21). Jesus knew that Judas would betray Him publicly.

However, someone else denied Jesus publicly. A second disciple decided not to obey the Great Commission. In truth, there were only ten disciples who remained faithful. So why did Jesus invite "eleven" to meet Him? I will teach you that the second disobedient disciple was reincluded, and that he obeyed Jesus's important command!

If we discount both disciples who betrayed Jesus when we read that He asked the "eleven" to meet Him in Galilee, then we would only have ten disciples. The math is off. However, this second disciple is Peter, and we must take a closer look at the story of his public denial of Christ.

The story of Peter's denial of Jesus is recorded in the Synoptic Gospels and the book of John. The Synoptic Gospels include only Matthew, Mark, and Luke. The inclusion of Peter's denial in all four gospels highlights the importance of his restoration. Judas and Peter both sinned and denied Jesus publicly. I believe that Judas was sorry for what he did. That may be a repentance of his mind (Gnosis), but not his heart (Yada).

Peter repented with his heart (Yada), and he was reincluded. Now we can understand why Jesus invited the "eleven" disciples to meet Him in Galilee. This was a public invitation that reincluded Peter. Of course, we all know that Jesus asked Peter if he loved Him three times, perhaps to match his three public denials. Matthew 26:75 says, "Then Peter remembered the word Jesus had spoken: 'Before the rooster crows, you will disown me three times.' And he went outside and wept bitterly." This verse shows a Yada heart repentance. Luke 22:61 says, "The Lord turned and looked straight at Peter. Then Peter remembered the word the Lord had spoken to him: 'Before the rooster crows today, you will disown me three times.'"

GOOD NEWS:
WE ARE ALL FORGIVEN AND REINCLUDED IF WE REPENT WITH A YADA HEART!

You need to realize the Great Commission is for everyone, even people who have strayed from their faith. Jesus made a tremendous sacrifice and loves you too much for you to walk in unforgiveness. If you have strayed, take a moment to ask Him to reinclude you. We must recognize God's love and forgiveness, and those things should motivate us to be and make disciples.

A very important and central scripture for T3D International is Matthew 28:19, "Therefore go and make disciples of all nations, baptizing them in the name of the Father and of the Son and of the Holy Spirit." Remember, "go" is not a command in this scripture. In this verse, "go" a passive verb that means "in your going." The command verb here is to systematically "make disciples" as you go. This is clearly what most Christians around the world are NOT doing.

Jesus spoke this command! What was He doing thirty-five verses before He spoke this command (Matthew 28:19 counting backwards to Matthew 27:50.)? I will tell you what Jesus was doing: He was dying on the cross.

Do you think Jesus gave this command so you can decide if you want to obey? If you have the time? If Jesus returned from the dead and His first words to His disciples were "make disciples," how serious is His command? What if someone you knew who had passed away returned from the dead and said to you, "make disciples"? Would that be a request that you would take seriously?

Matthew 28:19 is at the core of T3D International. It also repeats the Trinity formula of Father, Son, and Holy Spirit, another core T3D idea. You will never find the word "Trinity" in the Bible, yet the Trinity formula is found throughout the entire Bible.

You will find that all important biblical teachings have roots in Genesis. The formula for the Trinity is found in Genesis 1:26, "… let us make man in our image." When God used the plural "us" and "our," He was including the Trinity. Matthew 28:19 becomes important to us because Jesus's command to make disciples is declared with the Trinity formula: Father, Son, and Holy Spirit.

When you find the Trinity formula in the Bible, it underscores the importance of the event that is being described. For example, the baptism of Jesus is found in all four gospels: it is described in Matthew 3:16, Mark 1:10-11, and Luke 3:21-22, and confirmed in John 1:29-34. When Jesus was baptized, the Father peeked through the clouds and the Holy Spirit descended on Jesus. Just as the presence of the Trinity confirmed the importance of baptism, the appearance of the Trinity formula in the Great Commission also marks the significance of Jesus's command. Belief in the Trinity is important to Classical Pentecostals and to the teaching of T3D International. This theology about the Trinity is the fundamental idea of T3D International.

We will all learn Mathew 28:19. "Go" (in your going) "make disciples." The Lord's blessings are on you in your going! Remember, you cannot "go" in the will of God and stay where you are!

A cute English language reminder is that the first two letters of God's name are "GO." The first three letters of satan's name are

"SAT." Whether you have decided to "go" or whether you "sat" on the sidelines depends on who you are following!

WELCOME TO T3D INTERNATIONAL, I AM SO GLAD THAT YOU ARE PART OF THE TEAM!

After you read each of the theological chapters, you will need to fill in the blanks of the T3D International workbook. The workbook will appear after each chapter. Each chapter workbook will need to be filled out before you graduate; this is one of the five requirements. Try to fill in the blanks using your memory. If you get stuck, the answers are in the previous chapter.

Chapter Four:
T3D International Workbook

After each of the following chapters you will find duplicate portions of the chapters with some blanks. Fill in these blanks using your memory of what you just read. If you have any difficulties filling in the blanks, go back through the chapter you read and find the corresponding words. The workbooks will only contain portions of the chapter. Filling in all the blanks is one of your graduation prerequisites.

The workbook begins below.

First, I will teach you a new T3D International greeting. I want you to make sure that everyone you teach understands this new greeting, which is called "I Am an _____."

Teach your disciples the importance of being an original. If you bought a _____ painting, it would cost millions of dollars. Why? Because if it is an original, it will cost more to buy. Consider what you are _____ . Though this is not an official theology, I believe that when God formed you in your mother's womb (_____), He signed you as one of a kind, an original, by giving you unique fingerprints!

God is _____ and forms each new creation without duplicating what He has done before or what He will form in the future. He designed enough combinations of loops, whorls, and ridges for an infinite number of individuals to be signed by Him!

Also, think about how God designed your _____ with your own personal characteristics. But not even identical twins, who have the same DNA, will have the same fingerprint. Of all the people who have lived, are alive now, and will be born, no two people have the same friction ridges and recesses on ten fingers and ten toes!

Now I want to teach you two essential terms: _____ and _____ . Do not worry about how cerebral the words appear. I will help you understand the meaning of every difficult word in this book.

The first word is "_____." This word is weighty. For now, let me help you understand how epistemology will be used for the T3D International discipleship training course. You need to understand that epistemology is the science of how we learn or know what we know at the present time. If we apply the science of epistemology, we can say that a child learns through _____.

The second word that is important to us is "theology." "Theology" is a combination of two Greek words:_____, which signifies "God" (who we find in the Old and New Testaments), and , which signifies "rational thought and the word." Simply defined, theology is the _____of _____.
This definition of the "study of God" will include the Trinity.

In this book, we will study God by considering His intimate _with us. I want to point out specific scriptures that show the Trinity's self-revelation and how it impacts our human experience. Of course, when we study the Word to study God, it is considered biblical theology. Remember that as we study Him, He is _____us.

In this book, you will learn key biblical theologies pertaining to T3D International discipleship. Each theology will explain a study about God and who He is in relation to training disciples. As you teach the theologies of this book to your disciples, the Holy Spirit and His Word will permeate your spirit.

Do not let the words "_____" and "_____" scare you. For now, the meaning of "Gnosis" is "_____," and "Yada" is "_____."

Jesus _____ His life to free the world from the slavery of sin. After Jesus's resurrection, His first concern was the Great Commission. The first command He gave to His disciples was "_____ and make _____." Jesus knew that making disciples was a mission that would show humans their true value and purpose in the world and allow them to develop a greater understanding of who God is.

In my book, you will learn that God is at _____ around you, that He believes in you, and that He is choosing you right now to work with Him to learn how to be a disciple and train three new disciples (who train others to be disciples). To be disciples and train others, we must be _____ of His word. Let me explain a chapter in Matthew using a Yada (heart) approach rather than a Gnosis (mind) approach. Now we will delve into a deep study of the theology of discipleship. Matthew 28:16-20 is a core scripture for T3D International. This scripture is commonly referred to as the "Great Commission." Many do not include Matthew 28:16, "Then the _____ disciples went to Galilee, to the mountain where Jesus had told them to go," in the Commission. I want to include this verse, as well as Mark 14:28: "But after I have risen, I will go ahead of you into Galilee." In Matthew, Jesus asked the disciples to go ahead of

Him to Galilee. The scripture from Mark talks about where Jesus would go after His resurrection…Galilee! This is exactly where he told His eleven disciples to go. Does that seem strange to you?

After the great display of power from the Trinity, Jesus urgently asked His eleven disciples to go and meet Him in Galilee. Whenever God says "go," He means that you are in one place, and He wants you to come to the place He wants. He wants us to constantly be in a place to _____ Him. This "go" is for sure connected to Matthew 28:19, which says "go and make disciples."

I also want to connect God's command to "go" with our early epistemologies. We may not have learned to obey His commands as children. We need to relearn how to "go." Our childhood experiences (from when we did not have the ability to _____ the _____) may not be enough for us to obey the Great Commission. Now, as adults, we are informed with biblical and practical experiences of who God is. We now have the ability to judge correctly. We are the ones who need to move when He says "go." "Go" does not always signify an overseas assignment (it can), but it certainly signifies moving from where you are—even if it is just moving across the street to talk to someone different than you. The meaning of "go" could be finishing this book and training other disciples around the world with T3D International.

Matthew 28:16 says that Jesus told the "eleven" to meet Him. One was missing. Who? I will not tell you right away. I want you to think about who was missing. Jesus asked eleven disciples to meet Him; I thought that there were twelve disciples.

You will quickly apprehend that _____ is missing. He is one disciple who decided not to do the Great Commission. Peter explained to the new church what had happened to Judas in Acts 1:15-20. I do not believe that Judas was _____ to die in sin; satan deceived him and he yielded to evil. Jesus came to rescue every living soul, even Judas. Jesus washed his feet. How can you not repent with Jesus kneeling in front of you, looking into your eyes while washing your feet? It was Jesus's way of saying to Judas, "I still love you; you are one of mine."

However, someone else denied Jesus publicly. A second disciple decided not to obey the Great Commission. In truth, there were only disciples who remained faithful. So why did Jesus invite "eleven" to meet Him? I will teach you that the second disobedient disciple was _____, and that he obeyed Jesus's important command!

The story of Peter's denial of Jesus is recorded in the _____ Gospels and the book of John. The Synoptic Gospels include only Matthew, _____ , and Luke. The inclusion of Peter's denial in all four gospels highlights the importance of his restoration. Judas and Peter both sinned and denied Jesus _____ . I believe that Judas was sorry for what he did. That may be a repentance of his mind (Gnosis), but not his heart (Yada).

Peter repented with his heart (Yada), and he was reincluded. Now we can understand why Jesus invited the "eleven" disciples to meet Him in Galilee. This was a public invitation that reincluded Peter. Of course, we all know that Jesus asked Peter if he loved Him three times, perhaps to match his three public denials.

GOOD NEWS:
WE ARE ALL FORGIVEN AND REINCLUDED IF WE REPENT WITH A YADA HEART!

You need to realize the Great Commission is for everyone, even people who have _____ from their faith. Jesus made a tremendous sacrifice and loves you too much for you to walk in unforgiveness. If you have strayed, take a moment to ask Him to reinclude you. We must recognize God's love and forgiveness, and those things should motivate us to be and make disciples.

A very important and central scripture for T3D International is Matthew 28:19, "Therefore go and make disciples of all nations, baptizing them in the name of the Father and of the Son and of the Holy Spirit." Remember, "go" is not a command in this scripture. In this verse, "go" a passive verb that means "in your going." The command verb here is to systematically "make disciples" as you go. This is clearly what most Christians around the world are _____ doing. Matthew 28:19 is at the _____ of T3D International. It also repeats the Trinity formula of Father, Son, and Holy Spirit, another core T3D idea. You will never find the word " _____ " in the Bible, yet the Trinity formula is found throughout the entire Bible.

You will find that all important biblical teachings have roots in Genesis. The formula for the Trinity is found in Genesis 1:26, "… let us make man in our image." When God used the _____ "us" and "our," He was including the Trinity. Matthew 28:19 becomes important to us because Jesus's command to make disciples is declared with the Trinity formula: Father, Son, and Holy Spirit.

When Jesus was baptized, the Father peeked through the clouds and the Holy Spirit descended on Jesus. Just as the presence of the Trinity_____ the importance of baptism, the appearance of the Trinity formula in the Great Commission also marks the significance of Jesus's command. Belief in the Trinity is important to Classical Pentecostals and to the teaching of T3D International. This theology about the Trinity is the _____ idea of T3D International.

Chapter Five:
Two Epistemologies: Gnosis and Yada

I want to further define the term epistemology in this chapter because I believe that to obey the Great Commission, we must evaluate the core of who we are. It is a possibility that we do not know how to make a disciple because making disciples was never taught to us when we were children. We need to examine ourselves and analyze if what we were taught about God coincides with His Word. Studying epistemology may help you with this evaluation.

Epistemology attempts to answer the question of how we know the concepts that we know. The word "epistemology" is derived from the Greek e*pistēmē* ("knowledge") and *logos* ("reason"). Most people are likely to cease their efforts at some point and be content with whatever degree of understanding they have managed to achieve. A person cannot reasonably be said to know something if he or she does not believe it to be true.

There are four main bases of knowledge: divine revelation, experience, logic and reason, and intuition. These four bases of knowledge are how we learn and interact with something new in our culture. Although a true scientific definition of epistemology will only include logic and reason as bases of knowledge, for this section about the definition of epistemology, I will modify the secular definition of the four bases of knowledge and view them from a biblical perspective. This will allow you to modify your epistemology and begin to train disciples.

How do we know what we know? From birth to adulthood, we "know what we know" through major social institutions: family, education, employment. We also receive more specialized learning from friendships, academies, and tribal activities. The activities we learn from institutions can appear to be good or bad behaviors depending on cultural perspective. An example of bad behavior would be motorcycle gangs. Whether you view a motorcycle gang as bad or good would depend on whether you belong to the gang or not.

The four main bases of knowledge are divine revelation, experience, logic and reason, and intuition. I will integrate the four bases after I give you an operational definition of each one.

In this course, "divine revelation" refers to the ways we hear from God and learn about His identity. Classical Trinitarian Pentecostals believe that as we enter an intimate relationship with God, He speaks to us in many forms. Although He does not often communicate in an audible voice, He speaks to us in many other ways. He even uses creation to communicate His will to us.

This is my personal example of hearing from God during my first week as a new Christian: I was having doubts about His love in my life. I was outside one night, parked in my old beat-up truck, overlooking a beautiful New Mexico valley. Exactly when I finished asking the Lord to let me know that He loved me, a shooting star appeared across the valley, leaving a tail as it burned out. I sat crying, as I am crying now (forty-five years later). I still believe that I serve a powerful and relational God. I knew that He loved me, and I know that He loves you! You can read about a powerful Biblical example of what I just testified about in the Old Testament. It was not a burning star; it was Moses when he saw a burning bush that was not being consumed. The point is that God is powerful, relational, and consistent in His word.

Religious institutions are one source of divine revelation. As children, we learn what we know from pastors, the Bible, churches, and members of churches. We also learn from the experiences we collect as we interact with these institutions. I believe that the Bible should be used to discern truth. The cultural interactions we experience from childhood to adulthood are not always informed by the Trinity found in the Bible. Most people do not learn in their early years how the Bible informs our lives. For this reason, reading the Bible is a core of T3D International training.

God's written Word is part of His divine revelation, and it is core to the teaching of T3D International. Most times as you read daily through His word, God will apply His word to your heart as if you read it for the first time. It will be fresh to you, and He will use His word to guide you. My hope is that through this book, you will sense His guidance as you study the theologies presented.

In the teaching of T3D International, the "experience" basis of knowledge will be called "Yada." The first appearance of the word "Yada" in original and relational language is found in Genesis 4:1. What appears in Genesis is important and often found throughout the Bible. The word "know" is "Yada" in the original language. For example, Genesis 4:1 says that Adam "knew" Eve and they produced a son, Cain. Adam "Yada" Eve. This sexual relationship between a man and his wife is the most intimate human relationship that we can experience. God wants a "Yada" relationship with you. I believe that this relationship is much deeper than a sexual one. Proverbs 18:24, 27:9, and John 15:15 confirm that He desires to be closer than a brother to us. He loves you in a deep way, even if it requires redemption that took the life of His only Son.

Logic or reason is another basis of epistemology. One of the Greek words that forms the word epistemology is *logos*. John uses the word *logos* in the first chapter of his Gospel to describe Jesus and the role of the Trinity in creation. The first chapter of John helps us see where Jesus is in the Old Testament. There is a definite logic to the Trinity, from the creation of the world to the shaping of your life and His future design for every individual.

Let me answer a thought that is on every mind. Where is Jesus in the Old Testament? Using the New Testament, I will reveal Jesus in the Old Testament. The New Testament says, in John 1:1-3, "In the beginning was the Word, and the Word was with God, and the Word was God. He was with God in the beginning. Through him all things were made; without him nothing was made that has been made." When we read "In the beginning," do not think that Jesus was created at this moment. The Father, Son, and Holy Spirit are who we refer to when we use the word "Trinity." Remember that the word "Trinity" is never found in the Bible, but that the Trinity formula is discovered everywhere in the Old and New Testaments (especially when you include these verses in the first chapter of John). The Trinity has always existed. Look at the language of these verses. The beginning of these verses shows that Jesus was there with the Father, and He is the Father.

When we apply John 1:3 to all the creation verses found in Genesis, it is revealed that Jesus was there during creation. He gave life to all creation. The Trinity was active during the creation. I would also like to challenge you to reread the Old Testament. As you read, apply John 1:1-3. When you come across the Father with the Holy Spirit, as you do in Judges 11:26 and 11:29, I believe that Jesus is also there in the Trinity Formula.

We are all originals to the Trinity. Remember the teaching I shared with you in Chapter Four: "I Am an Original." God's entire plan throughout His word is to love and save His creation. I challenge you to systematically read His Word every day.

Intuition is the fourth and final basis of epistemology. Humanly, intuition is a gut feeling that may or may not be based on years of learning and experience. "Love at first sight" is a phrase that demonstrates a form of intuition. Divine revelation can appear as intuition as you bathe yourself in God's Word. Years of experience, study of His word, and intimate relationship with God can lead you to "knowing His voice." We will follow His voice and do His will as we continue in the relationship. Often, as we personally live His Word, we will discern His will and obey it.

I want to give you some examples of my personal epistemologies—how I know what I know, things that I learned as I interacted with my different cultures. As a child, I was taught that it was wrong to cross in the middle of the street. This teaching was imparted with cute TV advertisements and jingles (that I still remember.) This concept can be learned and practiced through experience, logic and reason, and intuition. On the coast of Ecuador, children are taught that it is bad manners to point at anyone with their index finger. Again, this concept can be learned and practiced through experience, logic and reason, and intuition. These examples are not culturally universal to all nations.

Gnosis and Yada are two types of knowing, especially when it comes to knowing God. There is a huge difference between "knowing about" Him (Gnosis) and "knowing Him," experiencing God (Yada). T3D International was designed by marrying the terms Gnosis and Yada. Gnosis is knowing a person because you have information about that person. Using this epistemology, you would say that I know God because I have information about Him. Yada is knowing someone because you have experiences with that person. You would say that I know God because I have heartfelt experiences with Him. Gnosis, or head-based understanding of discipleship, will come as you read through God's Word and this book. As you transform through T3D International teaching, you will blend in Yada, a heartfelt experience found in my book. You will work on Yada as you complete all the experiential requirements for this study such as reading God's Word with a heart understanding, systematically praying for your disciples, sharing life's joys and sorrows with your disciples, training your disciples, and completing your Social/Evangelistic Project.

Using Gnosis, some of you were taught as a child to "know about" God from the information you received about Him, whether through divine revelation, experiences with Him, logic and reason, intuition, or all four bases at once. Maybe you received some correct instruction about God and His Word. Later in life, you intuitively made decisions about God based on your learning. If you did not have a Yada relationship with God correctly based on His Word, then how can you make followers for Him who teach others to follow Him? As I mentioned in Chapter Two, the serendipitous finding of my research data was that my two case study groups consumed the power of the Holy Spirit. These hundred people were trained through religious institutions as Pentecostals, and I still needed to teach them how to love and give to others. The Trinity demonstrates how to do this through the Bible as He loves and gives to us.

It is obvious that many people have learned to care about themselves. Making one disciple shows that you care about that person. The process of training a T3D disciple begins with learning about a relational God.

When I see so many around the world who have never systematically made a disciple, my heart weeps. We need to learn to make disciples with the Yada the Trinity communicates to us. How can they learn if nobody teaches them?

Some would say, "I already know how to train disciples through the information I learned about discipleship." That is Gnosis language. If you learned how to make a disciple by reading a book about making disciples, how many disciples have you made since you read that book? Are you making disciples now?

It is possible that you have never systematically formed a disciple who is now forming other disciples. I want to try a great experiment, to train you using both Gnosis and Yada, so you experience God with both your mind and your heart. I want you to learn to love Him like He loves you. As you learn that kind of love, I want you to focus His love toward others. T3D International represents a systematic way of breaking down what we thought we knew about God so that we can rebuild our epistemology, informed with Trinitarian knowledge. This process can feel uncomfortable. It is always uncomfortable to change a concept that we have held all our lives, even if some of our concepts are not true. We learned them as a child before we had enough reason to rightly discern the truth.

You may have read many books about making disciples. You have learned that it is important to make disciples. You know the steps, yet you have never systematically trained a disciple. I believe that it is not enough to know *about* discipleship, you need to know *how* to make a disciple. To learn how to make a disciple, I believe that you need to learn anew using the two epistemologies Gnosis and Yada. A leader's job is to teach you not only that it is important to make a disciple, but also how to make a disciple through new experiences and scriptural revelations. It is my prayer that before you finish this book, I can teach you "how" to make disciples by combining Gnosis and Yada. I do not believe that you can make disciples using only one of these two epistemologies.

You will learn to make disciples using all four bases of knowledge divine revelation (reading God's Word), experiences you will gain with your team and with the Lord, information about discipleship, and collective intuition. Reading this book, reading God's word, and learning Trinitarian theology will constitute a Gnosis approach to disciple making, while interacting with other disciples and completing the Social/Evangelistic Project will allow you to practice a Yada approach. As you follow my outlined steps, you will receive both new information and new experiences.

As you understand by now, my premise is that most discipleship programs are taught with the classic definition of Gnosis—knowing by using learned information, logic, and reason. Many people have read about making disciples from great books and programs. We have information about making disciples, but why are we not making them? What if in your formative years of learning you were not taught to consider a living God who seeks an intimate relationship with you? Exodus 34:14c says that the Lord, "… is a God who is jealous about his relationship with you" (NLT).

I want to marry the epistemologies of Gnosis and Yada. For our Yada epistemology, we will use the four bases of knowledge, biblically enriched. We will use the biblical understanding of reason and logic based on the logos of our Father and Jesus. Reason as given by the Trinity allows us to understand that creation speaks about God. Instead of reading a scripture engaging only your mind, try also engaging your heart. Think about a forest. Genesis 1:12 says that God created trees. The fact that trees still exist speaks about His love, omniscience, and omnipotence.

The experience basis of knowledge will take the form of heartfelt experiences with the Trinity through the Old and New Testaments and an active relationship with God as we daily seek to understand Him. The intuition component will not come from what we have learned, but from what we learn about God as we are in a relationship with Him. We will also experience divine revelation through the new relationship we have fostered with Him. God speaks and reveals His Word when we daily seek His heart through reading and obeying His Word.

These Yada experiences will be coupled with practical, hands-on assignments that you will "do." "Doing" involves experiences. I have asked over 1,200 T3D International students if they knew God. They all responded with a yes. So I asked them, "If you know Him, then what is His favorite color?" Nobody knew. Of course, this is a trick question because a favorite color could be Gnosis-based piece of information, and God did not give that information to us in His Word. The point is, we do not have such an intimate relationship with

God that we know His favorite things (if He has favorite things). It is possible that you know about Him (Gnosis), but you do not know Him (Yada) through revelation, experience, logic, and intuition. Of all the things that we can learn in God's Word, His favorite color may not be the most important. Let us look at someone in your family or among your friends. You find out about a favorite color by spending a lot of time with someone; through intuition (you see the color expressed in clothing or things around them); or by speaking to them (you ask them directly). You may not know God's favorite color, but you will find a much deeper experiential (Yada) relationship with God by applying similar epistemological approaches: spending more time with Him, speaking more with Him, and reading and obeying His word.

An example in the Bible might indicate how a group of ministers learned what they know in ministry, but without the involvement of the Trinity. This is one of the New Testament scriptures I fear most. I am not sure where the leaders in this Bible verse learned how to minister. Was it through experiences with other Christians, or from logic and reason as these men studied the Old Testament with other leaders? Was it by observing the life of Christ? The following text reveals a scriptural truth about the difference between Gnosis and Yada.

Matthew 7:21-23 says, "Not everyone who says to me, 'Lord, Lord,' will enter the kingdom of heaven, but only the one who does the will of my Father who is in heaven. Many will say to me on that day, 'Lord, Lord, did we not prophesy in your name and in your name drive out demons and perform many miracles?' Then I will tell them plainly, 'I never knew you. Away from me, you evildoers!'"

This scripture makes me fearful as I ponder the consequences of doing Gnosis-based ministry that stems from mind-based religious training. The people in this scripture called Jesus Lord, but they did not know that He did not "know" them. The Greek word the Lord uses for "know" is *ginōskō*. This word means "to learn to know [or] come to know," and is also a "Jewish idiom for sexual intercourse between a man and a woman."[5] This New Testament Greek word is like the Old Testament Hebrew word Yada. In Genesis 4:1, Yada describes the most intimate relationship between a man and a woman, representing the deeper relationship that the Trinity wants with us.

The men in Matthew 7:21-23 had information about who God was, what He did, and what He wanted—but they never had an intimate Yada relationship with Him. He did not know them! Luke 6:46 also says, "Why do you call me, 'Lord, Lord,' and do not do what I say?" Jesus cast those who were doing the correct religious things away.

I find it curious that we read in Jeremiah 1:5 that God knew us (Yada) in the womb and formed us before we were born. How is it possible that in Matthew 7:21 He no longer knows us? What happened? Jeremiah 1:5 tells us that God knew each of us in the womb. Something has happened during our maturing years, and we have become more Gnosis-focused and information-oriented through the world's style of teaching. The issue is that we act on what we have learned.

The Jewish people have cultivated Yada, heartfelt experiences with God, from the creation of the world to the burning bush to today. The elders teach the younger generation what the Bible calls the "Shema" in Deuteronomy chapter six. I believe that the Gentiles have left behind the Yada heartfelt experience of who God is and how He deeply loves us. You should know God because you spend intimate time with Him in His Word and in prayer. We learn in these verses that those who do the will of the Father will be known by Him. What is the will of the Trinity? The Trinity asks us to obey His commands in many places in the Old and New Testaments.

In this book I am highlighting a specific command made by Jesus: "make disciples." Rest assured that you are doing His will as you start systematically training other disciples with T3D International. He says in Matthew 7:21 that if you do His command, He knows you!

You need to read the scriptures daily from both a mental and relational perspective. God has been looking for an intimate and

---

[5] "Thayer's Greek Lexicon: Ginosko," BibleTools, accessed July 23, 2023, https://www.bibletools.org/index.cfm/fuseaction/Lexicon.show/ID/G1097/ginosko.htm.

loving relationship with each of His own since the beginning of time. I want you to start seeing the scriptures as coming from a living and relational God who loves you. Use a different lens, meditate on the scriptures. Use a Yada heart to understand how much He loves you. Luke 12:21 says, "Yes, a person is a fool to store up earthly wealth but not have a rich relationship with God" (NLT). There is no value in storing up earthly wealth and not have a rich relationship with God.

Having wealth and not Yada is the issue. Consider the birds, as Jesus told his disciples to do in Luke 12:22-26. "Turning to his disciples, Jesus said, 'That is why I tell you not to worry about everyday life—whether you have enough food to eat or enough clothes to wear. For life is more than food, and your body more than clothing. Look at the ravens. They don't plant or harvest or store food in barns, for God feeds them. And you are far more valuable to him than any birds! Can all your worries add a single moment to your life? And if worry can't accomplish a little thing like that, what's the use of worrying over bigger things?'" Keep reading God's Word daily so you can have a deep consciousness of who He is both mentally and relationally.

How many sparrows are there currently in the world? Are there half a million, or half a billion? If you see this scripture with a Yada heart, you will be filled with the peace of the Trinity knowing that He feeds every one of them each day, and that you are more valuable than one sparrow.

Wherever you are around the world, have you ever gone past a low tree branch and heard a sparrow in despair, walking up and down the branch saying, "Where am I going to get enough food to eat today?" That would be ludicrous! The purpose of this scripture in Luke 12 is to illustrate the futility of worrying about a basic need. Around the world, many worry rather than invoke an intimate relationship with the omnipotent God. Sparrows must wonder if we Yada-know God. You know God because you have spent intimate time with Him by reading His Word, talking to Him, obeying Him, and experiencing His characteristics. You are learning to see His Word through the T3D International Yada lens.

The Old Testament is very clear about what God set up as a sacrificial system. He started His preferred system for addressing sin as early as

Genesis. Do you remember that Adam used a fig leaf to hide his sin? God gave Adam the skin of an animal to cover his sin. In God's system, blood is required—but not the blood of lame and blind animals. To be worthy, the sacrifice had to be perfect.

Let's use a hypothetical story set in the time of the Old Testament and talk about a baby lamb and God's sacrificial system. Suppose that in the days of the Old Testament, a father gives his son a baby lamb to raise (crying, "baaah, baaah!"). The lamb follows the boy because he cares for the lamb in every way! One day, after many years, the father is showing the family what a blood sacrifice is. He asks the boy to bring the full-grown lamb to be used as the sacrifice. With tears, the boy brings his lamb to the father asking, "why my lamb?" There are many moments in the Bible when Godly events cause you to ask questions about who God is and why He does what He does? Many times, the Yada question is asked in the Bible by children and those being trained by their parents as the Shema teaches. The father tells his son, "Your lamb is perfect without blemish!" The father informs the boy exactly what each of us needs to become to be presented to God: a perfect and unblemished sacrifice.

Of course, this illustration hints that one day, God will give a perfect sacrifice for us: His only Son, Jesus. He demands a perfect sacrifice because He only gives a perfect sacrifice to us! Jesus is God's perfect sacrifice. John 1:29 says, "The next day John saw Jesus coming toward Him, and said, 'Look, the Lamb of God, who takes away the sin of the world!'" Jesus paid the extreme price to redeem you. His sacrifice allows you to know His Yada relational love for you. Understanding that love and sacrifice allows you to know that you are an original.

Chapter Five:
T3D International Workbook

Please fill in the blanks.

I want to further define the term epistemology in this chapter because I believe that to obey the _____ , we must evaluate the core of who we are. It is a possibility that we do not know how to make a disciple because making disciples was never taught to us when we were children. We need to _____ ourselves and analyze if what we were taught about God coincides with His Word. Studying epistemology may help you with this evaluation.

Epistemology attempts to answer the question of how we know the concepts that we know. The word "epistemology" is derived from the Greek _____ ("knowledge") and _____ ("reason"). There are four main bases of knowledge: divine revelation, experience, logic and reason, and intuition. These four bases of knowledge are how we learn and interact with something new in our culture. Although a true _____ definition of epistemology will only include logic and reason as bases of knowledge.

How do we know what we know? From birth to adulthood, we "know what we know" through major social institutions: family, _____, employment. We also receive more specialized learning from friendships, academies, and tribal activities.

The four main bases of knowledge are divine revelation, experience, logic and reason, and intuition. I will integrate the four bases after I give you an operational definition of each one.

In this course, "divine revelation" refers to the ways we hear from God and learn about His identity. Classical Trinitarian Pentecostals believe that as we enter an intimate relationship with God, He _____ to us in many forms. Although He does not often communicate in an voice, He speaks to us in many other ways. He even uses creation to communicate His will to us.

Religious institutions are one source of divine revelation. As children, we learn what we know from pastors, the Bible, churches, and members of churches. We also learn from the _____ we collect as we interact with these institutions. I believe that the _____ should be used to discern truth. The cultural interactions we experience from childhood to adulthood are not always informed by the _____ found in the Bible. Most people do not learn in their early years how the Bible informs our lives. For this reason, reading the Bible is a core of T3D International training.

God's written _____ is part of His divine revelation, and it is core to the teaching of T3D International. Most times as you read daily through His word, God will apply His word to your _____ as if you read it for the first time. It will be fresh to you, and He will use His word to guide you. My hope is that through this book, you will sense His guidance as you study the theologies presented.

In the teaching of T3D International, the "experience" basis of knowledge will be called "_____." The first appearance of the word "Yada" in original and relational language is found in . What appears in Genesis is important and often found throughout the Bible. The word "know" is "Yada" in the original language. For example, Genesis 4:1 says that Adam "_____" Eve and they produced a son, Cain. Adam "Yada" Eve. This sexual relationship between a man and his wife is the most _____ human relationship that we can experience. God wants a "Yada" relationship with you.

Logic or reason is another basis of epistemology. One of the Greek words that forms the word epistemology is *logos* . John uses the word *logos* in the first chapter of his Gospel to describe Jesus and the role of the Trinity in creation. The first chapter of John helps us see where Jesus is in the Old Testament. There is a definite logic to the Trinity, from the _____ of the world to the shaping of your life and His future design for every individual.

Let me answer a thought that is on every mind. Where is Jesus in the Old Testament? Using the New Testament, I will reveal Jesus in the Old Testament. The New Testament says, in John _____, "In the beginning was the Word, and the Word was with God, and the Word was God. He was with God in the beginning. Through him all things were made; without him nothing was made that has been made." When we read "In the beginning," do not think that Jesus _____at this moment. The Father, Son, and Holy Spirit are who we refer to when we use the word "Trinity." Remember that the word "Trinity" is never found in the Bible, but that the Trinity formula is discovered _____ in the Old and New Testaments (especially when you include these verses in the first chapter of John).

When we apply John 1:3 to all the creation verses found in Genesis, it is revealed that Jesus was there during creation. He gave life to all creation. The Trinity was active during the creation.

Intuition is the fourth and final basis of epistemology. Humanly, intuition is a gut feeling that may or may not be based on years of learning and experience. "Love at first sight" is a phrase that demonstrates a form of intuition.

Gnosis and Yada are two types of knowing, especially when it comes to knowing God. There is a huge _____ between "knowing about" Him (Gnosis) and "knowing Him," experiencing God (Yada). T3D International was designed by _____ the terms Gnosis and Yada. Gnosis is knowing a person because you have information about that person. Using this epistemology, you would say that I know God because I have information about Him. Yada is knowing someone because you have experiences with that person. You would say that I know God because I have _____ experiences with Him. Gnosis, or head-based understanding of discipleship, will come as you read through God's Word and this book.

Using Gnosis, some of you were taught as a child to "know _____" God from the information you received about Him, whether through divine revelation, experiences with Him, logic and reason, intuition, or all four bases at once. Maybe you received some correct instruction about God and His Word. Later in life, you _____ made decisions about God based on your learning. If you did not have a

Yada relationship with God correctly based on His Word, then how can you make followers for Him who teach others to follow Him?

Some would say, "I already know how to train _____ through the information I learned about discipleship." That is Gnosis language. If you learned how to make a disciple by _____ a book about making disciples, how many disciples have you made since you read that book? Are you making disciples now?

A leader's job is to teach you not only that it is _____ to make a disciple, but also ____ to make a disciple through new experiences and revelations. It is my prayer that before you finish this book, I can teach you "_____" to make disciples by combining Gnosis and Yada.

As you understand by now, my premise is that _____ discipleship programs are taught with the classic definition of Gnosis— knowing by using learned information, logic, and reason. Many people have _____ about making disciples from great books and programs. We have information about making disciples, but why are we not making them? What if in your formative years of learning you were not taught to consider a living God who seeks an intimate relationship with you?

An example in the Bible might indicate how a group of ministers learned what they know in ministry, but without the _____ of the Trinity. This is one of the New Testament scriptures I fear most. I am not sure where the leaders in this Bible verse _____ how to minister. Was it through experiences with other Christians, or from logic and reason as these men studied the Old Testament with other leaders? Was it by observing the life of Christ? The following text reveals a scriptural truth about the difference between Gnosis and Yada.

Matthew 7:21-23 says, "Not everyone who says to me, 'Lord, Lord,' will enter the kingdom of heaven, but only the one who does the _____ of my Father who is in heaven. Many will say to me on that day, 'Lord, Lord, did we not prophesy in your name and in your name drive out demons and perform many miracles?' Then I will tell them plainly, 'I _____ knew you. Away from me, you _____!'"

This scripture makes me fearful as I ponder the _____ of doing Gnosis-based ministry that stems from mind-based religious training. The people in this scripture called Jesus Lord, but they did not know that He did not "_____" them. The Greek word the Lord uses for "know" is _____. This word means "to learn to know [or] come to know," and is also a "Jewish idiom for sexual intercourse between a man and a woman."[6] This New Testament Greek word is like the Old Testament _____ word Yada. In Genesis 4:1, Yada describes the most intimate relationship between a man and a woman, representing the deeper relationship that the Trinity wants with us. The men in Matthew 7:21-23 had information about who God was, what He did, and what He wanted—but they never had an intimate Yada _____ with Him. He did not know them!

---

[6] "Thayer's Greek Lexicon: Ginosko," BibleTools, accessed July 23, 2023, https://www.bibletools.org/index.cfm/fuseaction/Lexicon.show/ID/G1097/ginosko.htm.

The _____ people have cultivated Yada, heartfelt experiences with God, from the creation of the world to the burning bush to today. The elders teach the younger generation what the Bible calls the "_____" in Deuteronomy chapter six. I believe that the Gentiles have left behind the _____ heartfelt experience of who God is and how He deeply loves us. You should know God because you spend intimate time with Him in His Word and in prayer. We learn in these verses that those who do the _____ of the Father will be known by Him. What is the will of the Trinity?

You need to read the scriptures daily from both a mental and perspective. God has been looking for an _____ and loving relationship with each of His own since the beginning of time.

The Old Testament is very clear about what God set up as a ____ system. He started His preferred system for addressing sin as early as Genesis. Do you remember that Adan used a _____ to hide his sin? God gave Adam the skin of an _____ to cover his sin. In God's system, _____ is required—but not the blood of lame and blind animals. To be worthy, the sacrifice had to be _____.

There are many moments in the Bible when Godly events cause you to ask _____ about who God is and why He does what He does? Many times, the _____ is asked in the Bible by children and those being trained by their parents as the _____ teaches.

God will give a _____ for us: His only Son, Jesus. He demands a perfect sacrifice because He only gives a perfect sacrifice to us! Jesus is God's perfect sacrifice. John 1:29 says, "The next day John saw Jesus coming toward Him, and said, 'Look, the Lamb of God, who _____ the sin of the world!'" Jesus paid the extreme price to redeem you. His sacrifice allows you to know His Yada _____ love for you. Understanding that love and sacrifice allows you to know that you are an _____.

Chapter Six:
Theology of Salvation

The theology of salvation will be taught in this chapter in a practical way. Why is this section a theology? Remember that I told you the simple definition of the word "theology" is the study of God. Before you continue to read, tell me how salvation is related to the study of God. Why is it a theology?

This chapter will present a biblical theology of salvation. This means that we will use the Bible to explain salvation. A study of God includes the salvation of His creation. Salvation is a main theme throughout the Bible. God rescues His creation. This chapter will be grounded in both Gnosis and Yada epistemologies. Many people read the scriptures to understand the Bible with their minds or to complete a Bible reading goal. The following scriptures will be taught to engage your mind and also create God's experiences of the heart.

This chapter includes information on how to evangelize because you will not have disciples to train if you are not consistently evangelizing. Your church needs a steady stream of new converts and disciples.

Whether you are reading this book individually or using this teaching to train T3D International disciples, everyone needs to learn the Romans Road to Salvation. Jack Hyles created this plan during his sermon on June 28, 1970. [7] Take time to learn his system, which I present in this chapter.

These scriptures are powerful for bringing a person who does not have an intimate relationship with the Trinity to salvation. They are equally powerful to help seasoned believers understand the plan of the Trinity for the evangelism of others. Consider Hebrews 4:12 and 13: "For the word of God is alive and active. Sharper than any double-edged sword, it penetrates even to dividing soul and spirit, joints and marrow; it judges the thoughts and attitudes of the heart. Nothing in

[7] Jack Hyles, "There Remaineth Yet Very Much Land to Be Possessed - Sunday Morning Sermon June 28, 1970," The Jack Hyles Home Page, accessed July 23, 2023, https://www.jackhyles.com/muchland.htm.

all creation is hidden from God's sight. Everything is uncovered and laid bare before the eyes of him to whom we must give account." The obvious truth is that God's Word applies to all His creation, those who need salvation and those who are already living redeemed.

I like many of the plans that exist to help people reach God's salvation. The Romans Road to Salvation is my favorite due to its simplicity. I will give you nine verses found in the book of Romans. I am only using one book of the Bible to help you. I will also give you two extra scriptures that are important to evangelism in books outside of Romans. In this theology, these verses can be used to bring an unsaved person to salvation. You will be given a free and practical method for memorizing these scriptures, and you will be given explanations for each of these scriptures. These are the scriptures:

- Romans 1:16
- Romans 3:23
- Romans 6:23
- Romans 5:8
- Romans 10:9
- Romans 10:10
- Romans 10:13
- Romans 10:14
- Romans 10:15
- John 3:16
- Revelation 3:20

How can you memorize these scriptures? First, let me prove that you are capable of quickly memorizing scripture. When I train disciples, even the most timid members of my class can memorize a verse I give them. I will use the scripture John 11:35: "Jesus wept." Do you think you've memorized it yet? That probably took you less than ten seconds. Anyone can memorize that scripture in under ten seconds.

Memorization is not about cramming important information into your brain; it involves spending more time with the scripture. For instance, take a moment to speak your home address out loud. How fast did you rattle out your address? How many weeks did it take you to memorize your address by repeating it over and over? You shared your house address with others. This is a form of learning that you can apply to memorizing the scriptures. A lot was involved to memorize your address and cell phone number, but you did it! Do the same with scripture: spend time with one verse, months if you want. I want to teach you some tools to use so you can accomplish the same results with the scriptures.

One method is to use index cards. You may not even remember what an index card is! No worries, you can also use a note app on your phone or text yourself. Practice this free system with friends and family, or even enemies and strangers. To practice with a friend, family, or even an "enemy," give the other person your index card.

Here is what you need to do prior to handing someone your index card: On one side of the card, write the scripture out. On the other side of the card, place the scripture reference in the middle. On the same side of the card as the reference, the cards will be numbered one to eleven (based on the order in which they appear on the list above).

Give the card to any person, even a stranger on the bus or wherever you are. Let the person know that a famous author of a book is pushing you to memorize scriptures and that you wonder if you could get some help with your memorization. Not many will refuse you. Let the person know that (s)he should look at the scripture while you speak it out loud, and ask him or her to check your accuracy and correct you if needed. Here is the catch: even if you can speak the scripture perfectly, mess up somewhere. The other person will read it out correctly to help you. As the scripture is read out loud, the Holy Spirit will cement His word in your heart and the heart of the other person too.

Tape the card to a mirror that you frequent. Before you leave the house, you should look into the mirror. When you look into the mirror, you need to look at the scripture card for T3D International and read it once or twice every day, until you can repeat that scripture by heart.

Always carry all your index cards with you, reading them until you know the scriptures by heart. You can even make a small ring of these scriptures that you can carry. Surround each card with clear plastic, put a ring hole in each corner, and put a ring through it. These protected scriptures will not get damaged, and you can carry them with you everywhere. You can get a set of prepared scripture cards through the T3D International merchandise store; information for the store is included in a section at the end of the book.

The amount of time you need to spend on each scripture is not important—hiding the scriptures in your heart is. Remember, the Trinity can bring to your heart and mind all the scriptures that you take time to hide. If you want to hide something, it will take time.

Use nonproductive time to read the scriptures. What is nonproductive time? Most people will say that they are too busy to memorize scriptures. The fact is, they believe they cannot memorize scripture, so they do not even try. Right now, if you can tell me your phone number or house address, you can memorize a scripture with my technique. It is more than likely that as you read that last sentence, you spoke out both your address and your phone number in your mind. If you take the time to write out one scripture on an index card and carry it with you, I guarantee that you will hide it in your heart as Psalm 119:11 describes. You will declare, "I WILL memorize scriptures."

So, what is an example of nonproductive time? Many people have a lot of time during the day. It is not a matter of how much time you have, it is more a matter of the priority you assign to the use of your time. There is no need to mention the hours people spend on social media. Let us consider time spent driving a vehicle or riding a bus. If we dedicate five minutes a day during those nonproductive times to the constant reading of the scripture on one card, it may not even take a week to memorize one scripture. Five minutes of work times seven days equals the memorization of one scripture in thirty-five minutes. If you couple this process with handing the card to another person to practice verbalizing the scripture, memorizing the scripture may even take less time. For now, only use your nonproductive time to memorize what you write on your index cards. In truth, you can and will hide His Word in your heart!

I used this method to memorize the Romans Road scriptures. I know the meaning of these scriptures at both a Gnosis and Yada level. I always use the Romans Road to Salvation to evangelize, and I always begin with the first scripture (Romans 1:16) and proceed to the last one (Revelation 3:20.) I never share the next scripture until the person that I am speaking with reassures me that (s)he understands the reference.

Each scripture in the Romans Road to Salvation will be explained below. Never continue to the subsequent scripture if there is any lack of understanding of previously taught scriptures. The goal is the sharing and understanding of the Word of God based on Gnosis and Yada experiences.

Now study these specifically selected scriptures in Romans.

1. Romans 1:16:

"For I am not ashamed of the Gospel, because it is the power of God that brings salvation to everyone who believes: first to the Jew, then to the Gentile."

"I am not ashamed of the gospel." Yes, you are ashamed of the gospel! This is the word of Jesus, why are you ashamed of it? Be honest with yourself. I have determined that you *are* ashamed of the Gospel. It is my thought that because you never share God's Word with anyone, you are ashamed of His Word in some fashion. I have made that same statement to over 1,200 students, unchallenged. When you start memorizing these scriptures, you will constantly say, "I am not ashamed of the gospel!" You will begin to believe this word and begin to share God's Word with others, with His anointing. In Luke 9:26, Jesus says, "Whoever is ashamed of me and my words, the Son of Man will be ashamed of them." Keep reading the Romans Road to Salvation. Pray and ask God to let you sense the love of these scriptures. You are not in a race, let this meditation take as long as you need. I guarantee you that the Trinity will unashamedly apply these scriptures toward an unredeemed soul at a precise time.

The verse continues, "[the gospel] is the power of God that brings salvation to everyone who believes." Power is the Greek word *dunamis*: miraculous power, potential or ability. In systematic theology, one of God's characteristics is omnipotence (this will be explained further in Chapter Nine). His unlimited power is found in the first verse that is used in the theology of salvation. I am not ashamed of the gospel because it is God's power. I am not afraid to share this scripture, because God will use it to open and enter the hearts of the people He wants to save. Do not worry, your job is not to save the souls of people. Your job is to share the gospel with others, and the Holy Spirit will save their souls. Be loving, friendly, joyous, and kind as you evangelize.

I am told that it takes sixteen to twenty-one touches to win the heart of a person to Jesus. We know that the Holy Spirit can win someone on the first touch. It is on the human side that someone may not accept the Lord right away. You do not know what number of the sixteen to twenty-one touches you are as you share the gospel with someone. You may be the precise person that individual needs to take that step of faith. Love souls and keep obeying His Word as you evangelize to others. Romans 1:16 plainly identifies that God's power will bring salvation to *everyone* who believes. Now that is power!

2. Romans 3:23:

"For all have sinned and fall short of the glory of God."

All. We need to be inclusive in the world we live in. This scripture is inclusive; it says "all." You can talk with any soul alive on this earth and look into their eyes and ask them if they have sin, and everyone will respond affirmatively. This is not my word; this is the Word of the Lord! We fall short of His glory. We are all in the same boat; we need a savior.

3. Romans 6:23:

"For the wages of sin is death, but the gift of God is eternal life in Christ Jesus our Lord."

What is a wage? It is future earnings from our own labor. If you work for anyone, you will receive a wage after a certain time. It is the same for sin: you will earn a wage. The enemy of our souls does not tell you about a wage until it is almost too late. We now know that the wage of sin is death. Death is what we earned for the sins we committed. Someone may ask, "how is it that I am not dead, even though I have sinned?" Good question. I have seen some young people die after a horrible car crash, driving while intoxicated. They died in their sin. Death is not always a physical death; it is also a spiritual separation between you and God. We can see this in the scriptures when Jesus was on the cross. Jesus walked this earth with no sin; He was perfect. Why then did Jesus say in Matthew 27:46, "...My God, my God, why have you forsaken me?" God loved and approved of His Son. I have heard that the Father, being holy, could not look on sin. Jesus bore all my sins on the cross of Calvary. He had all the sins of the world on His shoulders at Calvary. If the Father could not look upon His own Son, where are we when we have earned death through the wage of our own sin?

But there is a gift. God loves to give you gifts. This gift can only be given by the Trinity; only the Trinity can give eternal life. Where we live that eternity depends on what we do today with the wages of death. Someone must die.

4. Romans 5:8:

"But God demonstrates his own love for us in this: While we were still sinners, Christ died for us."

This scripture amazes me. Many say, "when I am clean from my sins, I will serve the Lord." When I was living in my sins on April 13, 1978, I thought the same until I read this scripture. God demonstrated His love for me by sending His Son to die for me while I was committing sin. How do you demonstrate love? There is no better way to demonstrate love than dying for another. Love is the only action that cannot be duplicated by the enemy. Think about this: Do you know a friend or family member who is a sinner? Could you send your own son to die for that person while (s)he is sinning? Would you? God loves you so much, He was willing to demonstrate His love for you by doing exactly that!

I am going to pause right here because you may feel the anxiety of conviction. Take a moment to allow the Trinity to accomplish His plan in your life. Pray. I am writing this book for you so that you can be a Christian leader who trains future disciples. If you feel the conviction of the Holy Spirit, take a moment and ask Him to forgive you. Make sure you teach your disciples to be sensitive to the leading of the Trinity.

Everyone must share the gospel so that everyone who believes will be saved (remember Romans 1:16?). In my mind, discipleship and evangelism go hand in hand. You will find this idea to be true when you complete your Social/Evangelistic Project. The purpose of this future project is to demonstrate the love of God to those who are lost. The Social/Evangelistic Project will be further explained in Chapter Twelve.

5. Romans 10:9:

"If you declare with your mouth, 'Jesus is Lord,' and believe in your heart that God raised him from the dead, you will be saved."

You must declare Christ's Lordship with your own mouth. You must believe with your whole heart that He was resurrected from the dead. You will be unequivocally saved.

6. Romans 10:10:

"For it is with your heart that you believe and are justified, and it is with your mouth that you profess your faith and are saved."

You believe with your heart—this is Yada. As Revelation 2:4 says, return to your first love, the place where God's "Yada" for you is evident. He is asking you to return to that position of mutual love.

You declare with your mouth. You must connect your mouth to your heart (Yada) and not just your mind (Gnosis.) You are saved.

7. **Romans 10:13:**

"'Everyone who calls on the name of the Lord will be saved.'"

With your mouth you must call out to God. You will be saved.

8. **Romans 10:14:**

"How, then, can they call on the one they have not believed in? And how can they believe in the one of whom they have not heard? And how can they hear without someone preaching to them?"

You must help the person in front of you to (Yada) believe with his or her heart, or how can that person call on Jesus? You must share the Jesus of the Bible, not the Jesus from your early family or social culture. You must share, or others will never have a chance to hear the gospel. God depends on you.

Imagine that an island of nine thousand people was dying of a rare disease. It was determined that in two years, if they did not receive a cure, they would all certainly die. A medical doctor discovered the cure. He was ashamed, never shared the cure, and the population of the entire island perished. What is your first reaction? I was outraged. Of course, this story was not true, but it is real as it concerns evangelism. The not-so-rare disease is sin; this disease has a one hundred percent spiritual mortality rate. You are the doctor, ashamed of the gospel. You have the cure. If you share the gospel, the people will be saved from sin. Remember that there is something worse than being lost without Jesus. The worst scenario is being lost without Jesus when there is no one to look for you! Set out to rescue the island. Win the lost at any cost.

9. **Romans 10:15a:**

"And how can anyone preach unless they are sent?"

You have a chance to share the gospel because you are being sent by the Holy Spirit via T3D International. Teach the army to preach His Word—the original disciples did! You are direct descendants of them.

Who will be behind you in ten years? Systematically, spiritually, and structurally, make disciples today.

10. Romans 10:17:

"Consequently, faith comes from hearing the message, and the message is heard through the word about Christ."

Everyone who hears the gospel will have faith to be saved through the power of God. This evidence is found in Romans 1:16.

After going through these scriptures with someone who does not know Christ, you can now leave them in a place of decision: is the person ready to decide to accept Christ, or will they leave Him outside? See this extra scripture that I am giving you.

11. Revelation 3:20:

"'Here I am! I stand at the door and knock. If anyone hears my voice and opens the door, I will come in and eat with that person, and they with me.'"

Jesus says, "Here I am!" He is present in the Word and He is present now as you share His Word with others. Imagine this scenario for a moment: You are about ready to sit down to eat a meal when you hear the front doorbell ring. You say to yourself, "great, who can it be?" So you peek out the front curtain and see that it is your best friend at the door. What would you do? People in most cultures would open the door and let the friend in.

I love including Revelation 3:20 when I share the Romans Road to Salvation because it leaves the person I am sharing with in a deciding place. They have heard that Jesus is a friend who sticks closer than a brother. Now they learn that He is standing outside the door. I have led them to this decision. Now I am asking this person, "What are you going to do? Are you going to leave your friend outside, or are you going to open the door and let Him in, into your heart?" I always inform the person that there is no door handle on the outside of the door. S(he) must open the door from the inside. If this is the moment that the Holy Spirit is going to bring eternal life, (s)he will be ready to open the door. I always ask the person if (s)he would like me to form a prayer of forgiveness for him or her to follow, or if he or she would like to offer that prayer personally. Frequently, I am asked to start the prayer. I am addicted to the experience of people closing their eyes as sinners and opening those same eyes as righteous people.

12. John 3:16:

"For God so loved the world that He gave His one and only Son, that whoever believes in Him shall not perish but have eternal life."

John 3:16 is a famous and well-known scripture around the world— just watch some sports and you will see signs with this verse in the crowd! I add it to the Romans Road to Salvation because it illustrates the Trinity's Yada love, Jesus's sacrifice, and our proper response. God loves giving you gifts. This thought comes to me after reading the Bible cover to cover forty-seven times over my forty-four years as a Christian.

You must get into the habit of reading God's Word every single day. I am convinced that the Jewish people have a collective consciousness of who God is. Remember, they teach the Shema to their children once or twice a day. Generation after generation, the Jewish people have obeyed the Word of God and have taught their children to have a Yada heart for Him—to know Him. What do we as Gentiles teach our children? To be careful with strangers? We need to have a collective consciousness of who God is by teaching our children to read and obey His Word every day. It is then that we will know that He loves us and that He is willing to show us that love by giving us His only Son.

You must believe. When we believe in God, His love will never tarnish. Unlike the love some have seen from their earthly fathers, His love is always perfect, and we can safely believe in Him. We can love Him back freely and completely without shame. If we ask, He will bring healing to our damaged hearts. My heart was severely damaged, and He has taught me the truth of a Father's love.

John 3:16 includes the phrase "eternal life" again. This time, there is a choice: perish or live. Someone must pay for our wage of sin. If we do not believe and choose what Jesus did on the cross, then we must pay for our sins. If we believe with our hearts and confess with our mouths that Jesus died on the cross of Calvary for us, then He paid the price. Someone must die; Jesus died so we would not have to. If you were being stretched out on a cruel cross to be nailed and hung to die, it is Christ who rescues you. While you were on the ground, your hands and feet ready to be nailed to the cross, Jesus heard your sincere cry, "Lord, please forgive me!" He picked you up, hugged you deeply, told you to go and sin no more, and took your place.

Remember that God is always a kind gentleman in evangelism. He will never force anyone to do something against the free will He gave them. Tell me what would be better: to bend someone's arm behind his or her back and say, "tell me that you love me," or to have someone you know come up to you and freely say, "I love you"? God loves when you tell Him that you love Him with your free will. Anyway, you cannot save anyone. Only the Holy Spirit can do that. You can share God's Word and His love in a practical way, and His Holy Spirit will do the work. This world needs kind and powerful people to evangelize in Jesus's name.

If you are working through this book as a team or in a devotional style, you may want to review Chapter Twelve sooner rather than later. I believe it is important to begin working on the Social/Evangelistic Project. At least review the chapter so you and your team can start brainstorming ideas for your project. In the meantime, keep reading and learning about T3D International. You need to begin looking ahead so you have a chance to complete your project before you finish the book. You and/or your team will need time to think of your creative Social/Evangelistic Projects that will elicit the Yada question: "Who is your God?"

Chapter Six:
T3D International Workbook

Please fill in the blanks.

The theology of _____ will be taught in this chapter in a _____ way. Why is this section a theology? Remember that I told you the simple definition of the word "theology" is the _____ of God. Before you continue to read, tell me how salvation is related to the study of God. Why is it a theology?

This chapter will present a biblical theology of salvation. This means that we will use the Bible to _____ salvation. A study of God includes the _____ of His creation. Salvation is a main theme throughout the Bible. God rescues His creation.

This chapter includes information on how to _____ because you will not have disciples to train if you are not consistently evangelizing. Your church needs a steady stream of _____ and disciples.

Whether you are reading this book individually or using this teaching to train T3D International disciples, everyone needs to learn the Romans _____ to Salvation. Jack Hyles created this plan during his sermon on June 28, 1970. [8] Take time to learn his system, which I present in this chapter.

---

[8] Jack Hyles, "There Remaineth Yet Very Much Land to Be Possessed - Sunday Morning Sermon June 28, 1970," The Jack Hyles Home Page, accessed July 23, 2023, https://www.jackhyles.com/muchland.htm.

These scriptures are powerful for bringing a person who does not have an intimate relationship with the Trinity to salvation. They are equally powerful to help seasoned believers understand the _____ of the Trinity for the evangelism of others.

I like many of the plans that exist to help people reach God's salvation. The Romans Road to Salvation is my favorite due to its simplicity. I will give you _____ verses found in the book of Romans. I am only using _____ book of the Bible to help you. I will also give you _____ scriptures that are important to evangelism in books outside of Romans. These are the scriptures:

- Romans 1:16
- Romans 3:23
- Romans 6:23
- Romans 5:8
- Romans 10:9
- Romans 10:10
- Romans 10:13
- Romans 10:14
- Romans 10:15
- John 3:16
- Revelation 3:20

Remember, the _____ can bring to your heart and mind all the _____ that you take time to _____. If you want to hide something, it will take time.

I know the meaning of these scriptures at both a Gnosis and _____ level. I always use the Romans Road to Salvation to evangelize, and I always begin with the first scripture (Romans 1:16) and proceed to the last one (Revelation 3:20.) I _____ the next scripture until the person that I am speaking with reassures me that (s)he understands the reference.

Each scripture in the Romans Road to Salvation will be explained below. Never continue to the _____ scripture if there is any lack of _____ of previously taught scriptures. The goal is the sharing and understanding of the _____ of God based on Gnosis and Yada experiences.

Now study these specifically selected scriptures in Romans.

1. Romans 1:16:

"For I am not ashamed of the Gospel, because it is the power of God that brings salvation to everyone _____: first to the Jew, then to the Gentile."

"I am not ashamed of the gospel." Yes, you are _____ of the gospel! This is the _____ of _____, why are you ashamed of it? Be honest with yourself. I have determined that you *are* ashamed of the Gospel. It is my thought that because you _____ God's Word with anyone, you are ashamed of His Word in some fashion. I have made that same statement to over 1,200 students, unchallenged. When you _____ memorizing these scriptures, you will constantly say, "I am not ashamed of the gospel!" You will begin to believe this word and _____ to share God's Word with others, with His anointing.

2. Romans 3:23:

"For all have sinned and fall short of the glory of God."

All. We need to be _____ in the world we live in. This scripture is inclusive; it says "all." You can talk with any soul alive on this earth and look into their eyes and ask them if they have _____, and everyone will respond _____. This is not my word; this is the Word of the Lord! We _____ of His glory. We are all in the same boat; we need a savior.

3. Romans 6:23:

"For the wages of sin is death, but the gift of God is eternal life in Christ Jesus our Lord."

What is a _____? It is future earnings from our _____ _. If you work for anyone, you will receive a wage after a certain time. It is the same for sin: you will earn a wage. The _____ of our souls does not tell you about a wage until it is almost too late. We now know that the wage of sin is death. Death is what we _____ for the sins we committed. Someone may ask, "how is it that I am not dead, even though I have sinned?" Good question. I have seen some young people _____ after a horrible car crash, driving while intoxicated. They died in their sin. Death is not always a _____; it is also a spiritual _____ between you and God. We can see this in the scriptures when Jesus was on the cross. Jesus walked this earth with no sin; He was _____. But there is a _____. God loves to give you gifts. This gift can only be given by the Trinity; only the _____ _____ can give eternal life. Where we live that eternity depends on what we do today with the wages of _____. Someone must die.

4. **Romans 5:8:**

"But God demonstrates his own love for us in this: While we were still sinners, Christ died for us."

How do you _____ love? There is no better way to demonstrate love than _____ for another. Love is the only action that cannot be duplicated by the enemy. Think about this: Do you know a friend or family member who is a sinner? Could you _____ son to die for that person while (s)he is sinning? Would you? God loves you so much, He was willing to demonstrate __ _____for you by doing exactly that!

5. **Romans 10:9:**

"If you declare with _____, 'Jesus is Lord,' and believe in your heart that God raised him from the dead, you will be saved."

You must declare _____ Lordship with your own mouth. You must believe with your whole heart that He was resurrected from the dead. You will be unequivocally saved.

6. **Romans 10:10:**

"For it is with your heart that you _____and are justified, and it is with your mouth that you profess your faith and are saved."

You _____ with your mouth. You must _____ your mouth to your heart (Yada) and not just your _____ (Gnosis.) You are saved.

7. **Romans 10:13:**

"'Everyone who calls on the name of the Lord will be saved.'"

With your mouth you must call out to God. You will be _____.

8. **Romans 10:14**:

"How, then, can they _____the one they have not believed in? And how can they believe in the one of whom they have not _____? And how can they hear without someone preaching to them?"

You must help the person in front of you to (_____) believe with his or her heart, or how can that person _____? You must share the Jesus of the Bible, not the Jesus from your early family or social culture. You must share, or _____ will never have a chance to hear the _____. God depends on you.

9. **Romans 10:15a**:

"And how can anyone preach unless they are _____?"

You have a chance _____ the gospel because you are being sent by the Holy Spirit via _____ International. Teach the army to preach His Word—the original disciples did! You are direct _____ of them. Who will be behind you in ten years? Systematically, spiritually, and structurally, _____ disciples today.

10. **Romans 10:17**:

"Consequently, faith comes from _____ the message, and the message is heard through the word about Christ."

Everyone who _____ the _____ will have faith to be saved through the power of God. This evidence is found in Romans 1:16.

After going through these scriptures with someone who does not know Christ, you can now leave them in a place of _____: is the person ready to _____ to accept Christ, or will they leave Him outside? See this extra scripture that I am giving you.

11. Revelation 3:20:

"'Here I am! I stand at the_____and _____. If anyone hears my voice and _____the door, I will come in and _____with that person, and they with me.'"

Jesus says, "Here I am!" He is present in the Word and He is present now as you share His Word with others. Imagine this scenario for a moment: You are about ready to _____ to eat a meal when you hear the front doorbell ring. You say to yourself, "great, who can it be?" So you _____ the front curtain and see that it is your best friend at the door. What would you do? People in most cultures would _____ the _____ and let the friend in. I love including _____ when I share the _____ Road to Salvation because it leaves the person I am sharing with in a . They have heard that Jesus is a friend who sticks _____ than a brother. Now they learn that He is standing outside the door. I have led them to this decision.

12. John 3:16:

"For God so loved the world that _____ His one and only Son, that whoever believes in Him shall not perish but have eternal life."

John 3:16 is a _____ and well-known scripture around the world—just watch some sports and you will see signs with this verse in the crowd! I add it to the Romans Road to Salvation because it illustrates the Trinity's Yada love, Jesus's _____, and our proper response. God loves giving you gifts. This thought comes to me after reading the Bible _____ to _____ forty-seven times over my forty-four years as a Christian.

Chapter Seven:
Theology of the Provision of God

God provides for His creation, and we can read accounts of Him doing this through the entire Bible. The Trinity wants to provide for you when you do not have what you need. In this chapter, I want to hone in on an important event where Jesus provided food for a multitude as He purposefully trained His disciples.

What can we learn theologically as we begin to understand how God multiplied two small fish and five loaves of bread? As you study His Word, you are going to hear God scream through every scripture, "I love you!" Jesus was concerned when five thousand men came to listen to Him and did not have enough food to eat that day. These people put Him first, even before their own food. God cares about our daily needs. If He feeds more than a billion sparrows every day, how hard is it for Him to feed you?

As you read the New Testament, you will find that some stories appear in all three Synoptic Gospels; as you read them, you will comprehend that the stories have varying details. Only a few stories will appear in the Synoptic Gospels and the Gospel of John. The two major stories found in all four Gospels are the story of the fish and loaves and the story of the resurrection of Jesus. I believe that when a story appears in all four Gospels, God has some important details He wants us to pay attention to. This is the reason I am teaching about the theology of God's Provision with the story of the fish and loaves.

Pay attention—I want you to notice the similarities and differences in the accounts presented in each of the four Gospels. The Gospel of John offers details of this story that are not listed in the Synoptic Gospels. The book of John may be written with more emphasis on the importance of relationships. Furthermore, Jesus is always presented as being in control in the book of John.

Before I teach you this chapter, I want to remind you about the teaching on epistemology that I gave in Chapters Four and Five.

Remember that epistemology is the study of how we know what we know. You learned (i.e., you were socialized in your culture) through major institutions such as family, school, university, work, etc. Most of the time, you learned things as a young child before you had the ability to judge if the information was correct. For the most part, you still believe (or repeat) the things you learned. Not everything you learned was wrong, but some things were, and some things were not taught to you completely. Now that you are an adult, I want to you to reevaluate one part of your epistemology: who God is for you. You have the benefit now of being able to make informed, adult decisions using theology and biblical references. You must weigh the material presented to you and make adjustments to what you know.

With this method in mind, I want to show you what Jesus did to change the epistemology of His twelve disciples. You will be reading the following event with both Gnosis and Yada. I will skew more toward Yada in my teaching so you can see some differences between a Gnosis and Yada reading. At times, we read verses just with our minds and miss all the fine, intimate relational information and background teachings of Jesus.

I will mention my epistemological teaching now so that you can see how Jesus challenges His Twelve as this story unfolds. We assume that all twelve disciples grew up as good Jewish boys. Each of their epistemologies was predictable. All good Jewish boys grew up the same—through great teachings, they learned the culture and customs of their Jewish world.

Jesus severely challenged (but did not criticize) what the disciples learned as children. He wanted them to add more to their learning as adults. Specifically, He wanted to add the truth of how the Trinity wants to minister to distressed people. Jesus did not want His disciples to minister with just their inadequate human capabilities. He taught the multitudes how much God loves to provide for those in need while simultaneously demonstrating an intimate relationship with His creation.

Jesus used this event, the multiplication of loaves and fishes, to correct His disciples' younger epistemologies to a more mature Trinitarian epistemology informed by both Gnosis and Yada. Jesus used a very stressful moment to break down old "knowledge" and allow the disciples to see new ministry possibilities. He is doing the same thing with you right now! Read the following chapter and keep in mind the points of Jesus's teaching and the epistemological challenges He makes to His Twelve and to you.

This theology will focus on the story of Jesus feeding the five thousand, found in the following scriptures: Matthew 14:13-21; Mark 6:31-44; Luke 9:12-17; and John 6:1-14. I am going to teach you from the Synoptic Gospels and the Gospel of John. My teaching will consist of explaining the scriptures in portions, starting with Matthew.

Matthew 14:13-21

When Jesus heard what had happened, he withdrew by boat privately to a solitary place. Hearing of this, the crowds followed him on foot from the towns. When Jesus landed and saw a large crowd, he had compassion on them and healed their sick. As evening approached, the disciples came to him and said, "This is a remote place, and it's already getting late. Send the crowds away, so they can go to the villages and buy themselves some food." Jesus replied, "They do not need to go away. You give them something to eat." "We have here only five loaves of bread and two fish," they answered. "Bring them here to me," he said. And he directed the people to sit down on the grass. Taking the five loaves and the two fish and looking up to heaven, he gave thanks and broke the loaves. Then he gave them to the disciples, and the disciples gave them to the people. They all ate and were satisfied, and the disciples picked up twelve basketfuls of broken pieces that were left over. The number of those who ate was about five thousand men, besides women and children.

With hearts filled with Yada wonder, we will look at this scripture.

Matthew 14:13a: When Jesus heard what had happened. Whenever we read phrases like this, we need to investigate the preceding scriptures. When we see a scripture starting with the word "therefore," we need to look at the previous scriptures to see why that word is there. What did Jesus hear? If you read the previous verses, you will see that Jesus had just learned that Herod had beheaded His cousin John. John's disciples buried his body and came to tell Jesus. How would you react to such news? The next verse makes sense, because solitude is a natural reaction to grief: "[Jesus] withdrew by boat privately to a solitary place." This theology shouts, "God loves us and cares about the emotional pain in our lives!" Jesus experienced emotional pain. He is teaching us that we need to take a private moment when situations crash around us.

Matthew 14:13-14: Hearing of this, the crowds followed him on foot from the towns. When Jesus landed and saw a large crowd, he had compassion on them and healed their sick. There are times when we need and want to get away to a private place. When compassion reigns in your heart, there are times when you cannot get away. Our compassion is directed toward the people to whom we minister. I believe that we need times to refresh, and God will give us those times.

Jesus took time to form His disciples "in His going." This event was unplanned and stressful, but Jesus used it as a teaching moment with the purpose of convincing His disciples to reevaluate and modify their youthful epistemologies.

Matthew 14:15: As evening approached, the disciples came to him and said, "This is a remote place, and it's already getting late. Send the crowds away, so they can go to the villages and buy themselves some food." Jesus's disciples were human and mostly thought within the limits of human possibility, rather than allowing the Holy Spirit to act first. They all saw that Jesus had achieved the goal of finding a private place—so private that there was no Hilton Hotel or McDonalds. Speaking from their human perspective, the disciples asked Jesus to send the people off.

How many people were there? We see from the title of the story that there were at least five thousand people who needed food.

Do not forget that Jesus and His disciples were also hungry! The disciples were not prepared for this task. You are a disciple since you are studying this course right now. You would more than likely think humanly before you trusted the Holy Spirit. I believe that the Trinity's favorite word is "impossible." When anything is impossible for us, the Trinity says, "I'm Possible!"

Matthew 14:16: "You give them something to eat." I can imagine how shocked you are right now. The disciples must have been saying, "Wait a minute! I believe that I did not hear what You said! You want me to do what? There are at least five thousand people in front of us!" Jesus used this as a teachable moment to show how humans in need join with the Trinity. We just do not get it at times. The Trinity wants to take an impossible human situation and show us what He can do. He will use impossible moments like this one to teach us His desired theology. Do you remember the first theology I taught you? Matthew 28:19 says, "go." I told you that in the Greek the word "go" is not a command; it means "in your going." The command in this verse is "make disciples." In the story of the feeding of the five thousand, Jesus is "making disciples" as He is "going." We as humans have a lot of His theology to learn as we become disciples and make more disciples. We need to exchange what we have learned about theology for the theology the Trinity wants to teach us.

Consider John 6:8-9: "Another of [Jesus's] disciples, Andrew, Simon Peter's brother, spoke up, 'Here is a boy with five small barley loaves and two small fish, but how far will they go among so many?'" In these verses, the disciples try to enter the realm of the divine, and they inform Jesus that they found five loaves and two fish. The disciples did not understand. Like us today, we do not understand what the Trinity is asking us to believe with our Yada heart. The disciples must have been thinking, "Jesus this is all we can find, five loaves and two fish. Do you see what You are asking of us? This is impossible. You want us to provide dinner for five thousand people? Do you see how ridiculous Your request is?"

Matthew 14:18: "Bring them here to me," [Jesus] said. The Trinity wants us to place our human hand firmly into His divine hand so we can see what is possible.

Matthew 14:19: And he directed the people to sit down on the grass. Taking the five loaves and the two fish and looking up to heaven, he gave thanks and broke the loaves. Then he gave them to the disciples, and the disciples gave them to the people. The disciples are trying to prove their human thoughts, but Jesus will show His miraculous provision in a human situation. You have some real situations that you face. You are not alone. Hebrews 13:8 tells us that "Jesus is the same yesterday, today, and forever." He will do something divine in your situation. Calm your mind (Gnosis) and engage your heart (Yada). He loves you.

In Matthew 14:19, Jesus does some very foolish and miraculous things. The first foolish thing that He does is ask for the five loaves and the two fish from His doubting team. He took from the disciples all the thoughts they wanted to use as proof against His impossible request. Jesus took their reasons not to believe and turned them into a reason for undeniable faith in the Trinity. As humans, we are more ready to deny the power of the Trinity than begin with faith in the Trinity. Jesus strongly wants us to begin with faith in the Trinity. I am sure that we have the same doubts in our lives as the disciples had. We try to give human proof that the divine plan of the Trinity will not work. Confess your doubts to God and ask for His divine clarity.

The next foolish thing that Jesus did was to have everyone sit down. I am sure that the disciples' hearts sank when they heard this request. In their minds I hear them saying, "No, do not ask the people to sit down!" In Uruguay or Ecuador, when you invite someone to eat, the cultural understanding is that you will pay for the meal. When the five thousand people were asked to sit down, they expected a dinner. Are you laughing in unbelief right now, thinking this is going to be a disaster? The phrase "sit down" committed Jesus and the disciples to a complicated and doubtful situation. Five thousand hungry people believed they were going to eat some bread and fish.

Jesus enacts a seven-step process in Matthew 14:19: 1) Jesus asked all the people to sit down, 2) He took the loaves and fish from the disciples, 3) He looked up to heaven, 4) He gave thanks, 5) He broke the bread, 6) He gave the food to His disciples, and 7) He allowed His disciples to distribute the food to the five thousand. Six of those steps Jesus accomplished, but one He allowed His disciples to perform. This was a seven-step process; usually, when we see the number seven in the Bible, it signifies completeness. Jesus invoked divine blessings on this impossible situation. These seven steps are only mentioned in Matthew 14 and Mark 6.

I only want to focus on steps six and seven because you may not have read them with your Yada heart. Jesus gave the pieces to His disciples after He broke the bread. We are getting closer to the full miracle, but this act alone is miraculous. Jesus broke the bread and gave it to the Twelve. You try breaking five loaves into twelve pieces—the pieces will be smaller broken. When there are five thousand people in front of you, breaking bread is not logical. Jesus wanted to make this a teachable moment so that the disciples (and us today) would never forget it. He put the broken pieces into the hands of His disciples! I am amazed when I read that Jesus accomplished the miracle using His disciples. The detail that Jesus put the miracle in the hands of the disciples is reported in only the Synoptic Gospels, not in the Gospel of John. I am not sure why the miracle being accomplished in the hands of the disciples is not reported in the book of John. What is important is that Jesus's divine miracle was accomplished in their hands. His disciples gave the bread and fish to five thousand hungry people.

Now what were the disciples thinking and feeling about this miracle? No longer doubtful, the disciples were probably thinking about how incredible their God is. When they talked with the five thousand as they gave them all the food they could eat, they probably talked up their Master: "Yes, my Lord is the best!" Jesus wanted to use His disciples to complete the miracle. He did not do this one on His own. Take a moment and look at your hands. I like to think about the moment each disciple had a little bit of food in their hands and gave food to everyone until they were satisfied. What did that feel like as the miracle took place?

This is a complete and unforgettable discipleship training moment for us as well. Think about it: you are His disciples, and He wants to allow miracles to occur through your hands today. Remember that this miracle is found in all four Gospels. Jesus looked to heaven, looked to the divine, and gave thanks for what the Trinity wanted to do in a humanly impossible situation. There was peace when Jesus controlled the moment. The Gospel of John often reports Jesus in control. He moved the moment from a human level to the miraculous level of the Trinity. Like in so many miracles in the Old and New Testaments, the invisible dominated the visible.

In 2 Kings 6:15-17, the prophet Elisha and his servant saw their enemies surround their city? Elisha told him, "Do not be afraid, for those who are with us are more than those who are with them," and the Lord opened the man's eyes to see His army. Greater is the one who is with us than the ones we can see. The invisible is mightier than the visible. I often ask groups to close their eyes and, in their minds, remove everything that was created. What is left? All the groups respond with "Nothing. Nothing is left." Of course, I tell them that they are wrong. The invisible is left. The Trinity is left, the Trinity has always existed. Most begin to cry when they hear the truth of this illustration.

Matthew 14:20: They all ate and were satisfied, and the disciples picked up twelve basketfuls of broken pieces that were left over. The number of those who ate was about five thousand men. The miracle continues—everyone ate and was satisfied! Twelve disciples collected twelve basketfuls. There was more food. Jesus does not waste food.

We have completed our analysis of Matthew; now I will examine the version of the story found in Mark. In the other Gospels' accounts of this story, I will only point out the differences from the Matthew account.

Mark 6:30-44

The apostles gathered around Jesus and reported to him all they had done and taught. Then, because so many people were coming and going that they did not even have a chance to eat, he said to them, "Come with me by yourselves to a quiet place and get some rest." So, they went away by themselves in a boat to a solitary place. But many who saw them leaving recognized them and ran on foot from all the towns and got there ahead of them. When Jesus landed and saw a large crowd, he had compassion on them, because they were like sheep without a shepherd. So he began teaching them many things. By this time it was late in the day, so his disciples came to him. "This is a remote place," they said, "and it's already very late. Send the people away so that they can go to the surrounding countryside and villages and buy themselves something to eat." But he answered, "You give them something to eat." They said to him, "That would take more than half a year's wages! Are we to go and spend that much on bread and give it to them to eat?" "How many loaves do you have?" he asked. "Go and see." When they found out, they said, "Five—and two fish." Then Jesus directed them to have all the people sit down in groups on the green grass. So they sat down in groups of hundreds and fifties. Taking the five loaves and the two fish and looking up to heaven, he gave thanks and broke the loaves. Then he gave them to his disciples to distribute to the people. He also divided the two fish among them all. They all ate and were satisfied, and the disciples picked up twelve basketfuls of broken pieces of bread and fish. The number of the men who had eaten was five thousand.

Mark 6:30-31: The apostles gathered around Jesus and reported to him all they had done and taught. Then, because so many people were coming and going that they did not even have a chance to eat... It is pointed out here that the apostles reported to Jesus all that they had done, and they did not even have a time to eat. Ministry is not easy. Besides the bad news Jesus received about His cousin, we can add that nobody ate—neither the five thousand nor

Jesus and the disciples. Retreating to a private place seemed like the correct thing to do.

Mark 6:34: So he began teaching them many things. The first verses that we looked at from Matthew reported that Jesus healed those who were sick. Here we learned that He taught them many things as well.

Mark 6:37: You give them something to eat." They said to him, "That would take more than half a year's wages! Are we to go and spend that much on bread and give it to them to eat?" Still thinking humanly, the disciples responded to Jesus by saying that feeding this crowd would take more than half a year's wage. Stop for a moment—how much is half a year's wage for you? This is a substantial amount in any culture around the world and a relevant question to ask. Your wage is what you earn for the year while you pay for the things that you need to survive in the culture where you live. If in Ecuador some earn $5,000 a year, half a year's wages would be $2,500. This $2,500 was to be spent in one night to feed five thousand people. In the Gospel of John, Philip reported that those funds would only give everyone a bite. Not many people can give that much money for a "bite" of food. This is a relevant thought for any culture, past or present, because half of a year's wages, whether you earn a lot of a little, is costly.

Mark 6:40: So they sat down in groups of hundreds and fifties. God likes order, and He sat the people down accordingly.

Mark 6:41: He also divided the two fish among them all. In Matthew 14, Jesus broke up the bread. Here, He divided the fish as well.

Now we will study this event through the eyes of Luke.

Luke 9:10-17

When the apostles returned, they reported to Jesus what they had done. Then he took them with him and they withdrew by themselves to a town called Bethsaida, but the crowds learned about it and followed him. He welcomed them and spoke to them about the kingdom of God, and he healed those who needed healing. Late in the afternoon the Twelve came to him and said, "Send the crowd away so they can go to the surrounding villages and countryside and find food and lodging, because we are in a remote place here." He replied, "You give them something to eat." They answered, "We have only five loaves and two fish—unless we go and buy food for all this crowd." (About five thousand men were there.) But he said to his disciples, "Have them sit down in groups of about fifty each." The disciples did so, and everyone sat down. Taking the five loaves and the two fish and looking up to heaven, he gave thanks and broke them. Then he gave them to the disciples to distribute to the people. They all ate and were satisfied, and the disciples picked up twelve basketfuls of broken pieces that were left over.

Luke 9:10-11: They withdrew by themselves to a town called Bethsaida. He welcomed them and spoke to them about the Kingdom of God, but the crowds learned about it and followed him. He welcomed them and spoke to them about the kingdom of God, and healed those who needed healing. In these verses, we learn the name of the private place. We know that Jesus healed and taught them, and now we know He spoke to them about the kingdom of God. I believe that the disciples intently listened to Jesus's teaching. The teaching about the kingdom of God given by the invisible would make for a different outcome to an impossible situation. Impossible only means "I'm possible."

I like the events written about in the book of John. I often share with everyone I meet that they should read the book of John. God has a way of using this book to share His heart with us. Let's see how the story unfolds in this Gospel.

John 6:1-14

Some time after this, Jesus crossed to the far shore of the Sea of Galilee (that is, the Sea of Tiberias), and a great crowd of people followed him because they saw the signs he had performed by healing the sick. Then Jesus went up on a mountainside and sat down with his disciples. The Jewish Passover Festival was near. When Jesus looked up and saw a great crowd coming toward him, he said to Philip, "Where shall we buy bread for these people to eat?" He asked this only to test him, for he already had in mind what he was going to do. Philip answered him, "It would take more than half a year's wages to buy enough bread for each one to have a bite!" Another of his disciples, Andrew, Simon Peter's brother, spoke up, "Here is a boy with five small barley loaves and two small fish, but how far will they go among so many?" Jesus said, "Have the people sit down." There was plenty of grass in that place, and they sat down (about five thousand men were there). Jesus then took the loaves, gave thanks, and distributed to those who were seated as much as they wanted. He did the same with the fish. When they had all had enough to eat, he said to his disciples, "Gather the pieces that are left over. Let nothing be wasted." So they gathered them and filled twelve baskets with the pieces of the five barley loaves left over by those who had eaten. After the people saw the sign Jesus performed, they began to say, "Surely this is the Prophet who is to come into the world."

John 6:1-2: Some time after this, Jesus crossed to the far shore of the Sea of Galilee (that is, the Sea of Tiberias), and a great crowd of people followed him because they saw the signs he had performed by healing the sick. The Gospel of John is very specific with the location. There is another specific reason the crowd followed Jesus. They followed Him because He healed them. He continued to heal them when they met Him at the remote place.

John 6:4-5: The Jewish Passover Festival was near....[Jesus] said to Philip, "Where shall we buy bread for these people to eat?"

The proximity of the Passover Festival is new information given in the Gospel of John. We also learn that Jesus was asking His questions to Philip. Can you imagine the thoughts that passed through Philip's mind? If you are reading these verses with me from a Gnosis epistemology, you will have similar thoughts. You need to read the verses and events of the Bible using a Yada heart. When you read His Word or hear the thing that He asks of you, you know from having experiences with Him that all things are possible. He is looking for you to say, "With me it is impossible, but with You, all things are possible." Philip was possibly thinking, "Maybe, Jesus you are overworked and need a rest more than we do." Philip's face demonstrated shock and disbelief. He must have thought, "Really Lord, such a desolate place? There are no bakeries or restaurants."

John 6:6: He asked this only to test him, for he already had in mind what he was going to do. I think this is the most hilarious part of the story in these four Gospels. Jesus only asked Philip about feeding the five thousand because He was just testing the disciples. Now that is funny. That is the last thing the tired, stressed, and hungry disciples needed to wrestle with during a discipleship moment.

This is exactly how we need to teach disciples. Jesus already knew what He was going to do! Present the gospel in a way that challenges what we think is correct theology. T3D International teaching has been testing what you believe theologically. A challenge we face is determining what the Trinity wants us to know from the scriptures. Some of the disciples that were with Jesus learned theology from Jewish masters, yet they still needed to be challenged with the theology of the Trinity. We must ask, "What does the Trinity want us to do, or how should we respond?" Then Jesus can teach us His correct theology. Sometimes personal stress is needed to push us to think—really think—about what the Trinity can do in each moment. We need to get away from our default religious behaviors.

John 6:7: Philip answered him, "It would take more than half a year's wages to buy enough bread for each one to have a bite!"

Again, you are reading that it would take half a year's wages to feed everyone. You may think it might not cost the same amount today. However, this is a relative amount. The cost would proportionally be as great then as it is now. We may only have an idea of what half a year's salary equals during John's time. What if we use our current time? For some, a half a year's salary could be five hundred thousand dollars. That is not my reality. That amount still would be a lot of money to give five thousand men a bite of food for one night. Well, you can imagine how well that would work. Most people would not even be willing to spend five hundred thousand dollars for a bite of food even if they had that much money to spare. Here is an important truth: Jesus thought that these five thousand hungry people were worth it. The Trinity believes that you are worth a miraculous effort.

John 6:9: Another of His disciples. Andrew, Simon Peter's brother, spoke up, "Here is a boy with five small barley loaves and two small fish, but how far will they go among so many?" Among five thousand people, the disciples only found five loaves and two fish. Really?! Out of five thousand people, that is really all the food that you found? If others in the crowd had food, they were not going to share with everyone else—a bit like today's world.

Another difference in the Gospel of John is that we have the name of another disciple. We also learn that the loaves were barley, and that the dinner came from a small boy. The Bible always provokes questions for me. That was a large dinner for a small boy. Maybe someone packed his dinner at home thinking the boy could share his food with another. This boy represents a family with kindness. Who would have thought ahead to pack a lunch for their child in a remote place? Going to the remote place was a spontaneous event, unplanned for the crowd. How did the boy get caught up in this crowd? Was his family with him? Was the food for all of them and the boy was allowed to decide to share it?

John 6:14: After the people saw the sign Jesus performed, they began to say, "Surely this is the Prophet who is to come into the world." The people saw the miracle and recognized Jesus as the prophet who had come into the world. It is very interesting that the detail of Jesus putting the broken pieces of bread and fish in the hands of the disciples was only mentioned in the synoptics. Jesus began the miracle and then allowed His disciples to participate in the distribution and recollection of the food for the five thousand people.

Now I want to share extra information that will absolutely challenge your theology further. In the Bible, it was the cultural norm to only report the number of men at an event. In this case, there were five thousand Jewish men. If you look closely at Matthew 14:21, you will read, "The number of those who ate was about five thousand men, besides women and children." So now it will be safe to blow your minds. Many scholars estimate the crowd to have included about ten to twelve thousand people, counting the women and children. The disciples (and perhaps you) were having trouble with the feeding of five thousand people, when really, the story was about feeding perhaps twelve thousand people! Reread these scriptures and tell me about the real magnitude of this miracle! Your God is all powerful! He is a loving and mighty God! He cares about the basic needs in our lives.

A separate miracle of the Lord occurred when He fed four thousand people using seven loaves of bread and fish. You can read about this miracle in Mathew 15:32-39 and Mark 8:1-9.

One of the Trinity's favorite miracles to perform is creating food. God creates daily bread for His people in both the Old and New Testaments. In John 6:32-33, Jesus relates Himself to His Father: "Jesus said to them, 'Very truly I tell you, it is not Moses who has given you the bread from heaven, but it is my Father who gives you the true bread from heaven. For the bread of God is the bread that comes down from heaven and gives life to the world.'" Jesus states that He is the bread of life. Do you need food right now? Stop and ask Him; He is able to provide. As you read through the Bible, see how many times miracles of food occur.

There is also an Old Testament miracle where the prophet Elisha fed one hundred people. 2 Kings 4:42-44 reports,

"A man came from Baal Shalishah, bringing the man of God twenty loaves of barley bread baked from the first ripe grain, along with some heads of new grain. 'Give it to the people to eat,' Elisha said. 'How can I set this before a hundred men?' his servant asked. But Elisha answered, 'Give it to the people to eat. For this is what the Lord says: "They will eat and have some left over."' Then he set it before them, and they ate and had some left over, according to the word of the Lord."

I want you to know that there are food miracles reported in the Old and New Testaments. Perhaps if the Trinity loves doing bread miracles, we should ask to be used when we are confronted with the hungry.

Jesus reminds us that He did these miracles in Matthew 16:9-10: "'Do you still not understand? Don't you remember the five loaves for the five thousand, and how many basketfuls you gathered? Or the seven loaves for the four thousand, and how many basketfuls you gathered?'" This scripture demonstrates two different bread multiplications. When you read the Word, you may think that there is an error. Jesus performed two miracles, one for five thousand men and another for four thousand men. In the miracle of feeding the four thousand, Matthew 15:32 mentions that the people with Jesus had been with him for three days without eating. The importance of these stories for T3D International is that they show how Jesus used His disciples in both miracles.

This is a very important chapter for T3D International because it confirms the core of what I am teaching. We may look at this story as if it was only about the Trinity doing a miracle of making bread and fish for twelve thousand people, supplying His creation's basic need. In my teaching, I affirmed that miracle and added that Jesus's goal was to transform the epistemology of His twelve disciples, teaching them to trust the Trinity first for divine results rather than relying on their human abilities. We as disciples are not omniscient, omnipresent, or omnipotent. Those characteristics belong only to God. I believe that we can trust the Trinity to use these attributes in our lives. I believe that Jesus found Himself facing the same concern about asking for the power of the divine to interact on behalf of others, while being completely human. I discuss this theological conundrum in Chapter Eleven; I hope you keep reading!

I want to create disciples who allow the Trinity to use them in this manner in our world with great needs. I wrote this book to raise awareness and start the process of training His Mighty Army.

Arise, Mighty Army

Chapter Seven:
T3D International Workbook

Please fill in the blanks.

God provides for His creation, and we can read accounts of Him doing this through the _____ Bible. The Trinity wants to provide for you when you do not have what you need. In this chapter, I want to home in on an important event where Jesus provided food for a multitude as He _____ trained His disciples.

What can we _____ as we begin to understand how God multiplied two small fish and five loaves of _____? As you study His Word, you are going to hear God scream through every scripture, "I love you!" Jesus was _____ when five thousand men came to listen to Him and did not have enough food to eat that day. These people put Him first, even before their own food. God cares about our _____ If He feeds more than a billion sparrows every day, how hard is it for Him to feed you?

I want to show you what Jesus did to change the _____ of His twelve disciples. You will be reading the following event with both Gnosis and Yada. I will skew more toward Yada in my teaching so you can see some _____ between a Gnosis and Yada reading. At times, we read verses just with our minds and _____ all the fine, intimate relational information and background teachings of Jesus. I will mention my epistemological teaching now so that you can see how Jesus challenges His Twelve as this story unfolds. We assume that all _____ disciples grew up as good _____ boys. Each of their epistemologies was _____ All good Jewish boys grew up the same—through great teachings, they learned the _____ and customs of their Jewish world.

Jesus severely _____ (but did not criticize) what the disciples learned as children. He wanted them to add more to their _____ as adults. Specifically, He wanted to _____ the _____ of how the Trinity wants to _____to distressed people. Jesus did not want His disciples to minister with just their inadequate human capabilities. He taught the multitudes how much God loves to provide for those in need while simultaneously an intimate relationship with His creation.

Jesus used this event, the multiplication of loaves and fishes, to correct His disciples' younger epistemologies to a more mature epistemology informed by both Gnosis and Yada. Jesus used a very moment to break down old "_____" and allow the disciples to see new ministry possibilities. He is doing the same thing with you right now! Read the following chapter and keep in mind the points of Jesus's teaching and the epistemological challenges He makes to His Twelve and to you.

This theology will focus on the story of Jesus _____ the five thousand starting with Matthew.

Matthew 14:13-2

When Jesus heard what had happened, he _____ by boat privately to a solitary place. Hearing of this, the crowds followed him on foot from the towns. When Jesus landed and saw a large crowd, he had _____ on them and healed their sick. As evening approached, the disciples came to him and said, "This is a place, and it's already getting _____. Send the crowds , so they can go to the villages and _____ some food." Jesus replied, "They do not need to go away. _____ something to eat." "We have here only five loaves of bread and two fish," they answered. "Bring them here _____," he said. And he directed the people to sit down on the grass. _____ the five loaves and the two fish and looking up to heaven, he gave thanks and broke the loaves. Then he _____ them to the disciples, and the _____them to the people. They _____ and were satisfied, and the disciples picked up twelve basketfuls of broken pieces that were left over. The number of those who ate was about five thousand men, besides women and children.

With hearts filled with Yada wonder, we will look at this scripture. *Matthew 14:13a: When Jesus heard what had happened.* Whenever we read phrases like this, we need to _____ the preceding scriptures. When we see a scripture starting with the word "therefore," we need to look at the previous scriptures to see why that word is there. What did Jesus hear? If you read the previous verses, you will see that Jesus had just learned that Herod had _____ His cousin John. John's disciples buried his body and came to tell Jesus. How would you react to such news? The next verse makes sense, because solitude is a to grief: "[Jesus] withdrew by boat privately to a solitary place." This shouts, "God loves us and cares about the emotional pain in our lives!" Jesus experienced emotional pain. He is teaching us that we need to take a private moment when situations crash around us.

Matthew 14:13-14: Hearing of this, the crowds followed him on foot from the towns. When Jesus landed and saw a large crowd, he had compassion on them and healed their sick. There are times when we need and want to _____ to a private place. When compassion reigns in your heart, there are times when you cannot get away. Our compassion is _____ toward the people to whom we minister. I believe that we need _____ _____ to _____, and God will give us those times. Jesus took time to _____ His disciples "in His _____." This event was unplanned and stressful, but Jesus used it as a teaching moment with the purpose of convincing His disciples to reevaluate and modify their youthful epistemologies.

Matthew 14:15: As evening approached, the disciples came to him and said, "This is a remote place, and it's already getting late. Send the crowds away, so they can go to the villages and buy themselves some food." Jesus's disciples were _____ and mostly thought within the limits of human possibility, rather than allowing the Holy Spirit to _____. They all saw that Jesus had achieved the goal of finding _____ a _____ place—so private that there was no Hilton Hotel or McDonalds. Speaking from their human perspective, the disciples asked Jesus to send the people off. How many people were there? We see from the title of the story that there were at least five thousand people who needed food. Do not forget that Jesus and His disciples were also hungry! The disciples were not prepared for this task. You are a disciple since you are studying this course right now. You would more than likely think humanly before you trusted the Holy Spirit. I believe that the Trinity's favorite word is " ." When anything is impossible for us, the Trinity says, "I'm Possible!"

Matthew 14:16: "You give them something to eat." I can imagine how _____ you are right now. The disciples must have been saying, "Wait a minute! I believe that I did not hear what You said! You want me to do what? There are at least five thousand people in front of us!" Jesus used this as a teachable moment to show how humans in need join with the _____. We just do not get it at times. The Trinity wants to take an impossible human situation and show us what He can do. He will use _____ like this one to teach us His desired theology. Do you remember the first theology I taught you? Matthew 28:19 says, "go." I told you that in the Greek the word "go" is not a command; it means "in your going." The _____ in this verse is "_____ disciples." In the story of the feeding of the five thousand, Jesus is "making disciples" as He is "going." We as humans have a lot of His theology to learn as we become disciples and make more disciples. We need to _____ what we have learned about theology for the theology the Trinity wants to teach us.

Matthew 14:18: "Bring them here to me," [Jesus] said. The Trinity wants us to place our human _____ into His divine hand so we can see what is possible. *Matthew 14:19: And he directed the people to sit down on the grass. Taking the five loaves and the two fish and looking up to heaven, he gave thanks and _____ the loaves. Then he gave them to the disciples, and the disciples gave them to the people.* The disciples are trying to prove their human thoughts, but Jesus will show His miraculous provision in a human situation. You have some _____ that you face. In Matthew 14:19, Jesus does some very foolish and miraculous things. The first foolish thing that He does is _____ for the five loaves and the two fish from His doubting team. He _____ from the disciples all the thoughts they wanted to use as proof against His impossible request. Jesus took their reasons not to believe and turned them into a reason for undeniable _____ in the Trinity. As humans, we are more ready to deny the _____ of the Trinity than begin with faith in the Trinity. Jesus strongly wants us to with _____ in the Trinity. I am sure that we have the same doubts in our lives as the disciples had. We try to give human proof that the _____ of the Trinity will not work. Confess your doubts to God and ask for His divine clarity.

The next foolish thing that Jesus did was to have everyone _____ down. I am sure that the disciples' hearts when they heard this request. In their minds I hear them saying, "No, do not ask the people to sit down!" In Uruguay or Ecuador, when you invite someone to eat, the cultural understanding is that you will pay for the meal. When the five thousand people were asked to sit down, they _____ a dinner. Are you laughing in unbelief right now, thinking this is going to be a disaster? The phrase "sit down" committed Jesus and the disciples to a complicated and doubtful situation. Five thousand _____ people believed they were going to _____ some bread and fish.

Jesus enacts a seven-step process in Matthew 14:19: 1) Jesus all the people to sit down, 2) He _____ the loaves and fish from the disciples, 3) He _____ up to heaven, 4) He ___ thanks, 5) He _____ the bread, 6) He _____ the food to _____, and 7) He allowed His _____ to _____ the food to the five thousand. Six of those steps Jesus accomplished, but one He allowed His disciples to achieve. This was a seven-step process; usually, when we see the number seven in the Bible, it signifies completeness. Jesus invoked divine blessings on this impossible situation. This is a complete and unforgettable discipleship _____ for us as well. Think about it: you are His disciples, and He wants to allow miracles to occur through your hands today. Remember that this miracle is found in all four Gospels. Jesus looked to heaven, _____ to the divine, and gave thanks for what the Trinity wanted to do in a humanly impossible situation. There was peace when Jesus _____ the moment. The Gospel of John often reports Jesus in control. He moved the moment from a human level to the _____ level of the Trinity. Like in so many miracles in the Old and New Testaments, the invisible dominated the visible.

Matthew 14:20: They _____ ate and were satisfied, and the disciples picked up twelve basketfuls of broken pieces that were left over. The number of those who ate was about five thousand men. The miracle continues—everyone ate and was satisfied! Twelve _____ collected twelve basketfuls. There was food. Jesus does not waste food.

Remember, I want to create disciples who allow the Trinity to use them the way Jesus's disciples were used and begin training to be part of His mighty army.

We have completed our analysis and questions of the Matthew account. Since the other three Gospels are similar, I will not add more blanks. Let's proceed to the next chapter.

Arise, Mighty Army

Chapter Eight:
Theology of Joy

How is joy a theology, a study about God? Joy is a condition of the heart, not a momentary emotion like happiness. Happiness is situational. A cake at a birthday party can bring happiness. Joy is a permanent condition of the heart that comes from faith in the work of God. In Nehemiah 8:10, the Israelites are told, "'do not grieve, for the joy of the Lord is your strength.'" Even in difficult times, the Trinity gives us joy.

I had to teach my students in Uruguay and Ecuador about personal joy. Joy is not prevalent in these cultures. Many people in the United States understand and express joy. This is not true in the cultures of Uruguay and Ecuador, and perhaps in other cultures as well. I am not an expert in these two cultures, but I have spent ten years as a missionary in Uruguay and twenty-two in Ecuador. In Uruguay, people even wear gray, brown, and black clothes. Colorful clothes were virtually nonexistent because it was culturally taboo to wear them. You can imagine the shock of a group of Uruguayan students when Denise and I showed up to preach in Hawaiian clothing and loud patterns, bright and colorful from head to toe. We sure learned about the Uruguayan culture that day when hundreds of people gasped at the same time! Spontaneous laughter and joy were rare. In Ecuador, you are prohibited from smiling even in photos for government documents. All documental photos reflect stoic faces.

I know that many cultures around the world are cruel and difficult to grow up in. Most people do not have an easy life. I believe that a theology of joy is helpful. Our joy comes from God. God speaks throughout the Bible about joy in ministry. Joy is based more deeply in the heart and endures longer than happiness. Joy comes from the Trinity, while happiness can be situational. Many times, the weight of life can produce tears. The Lord can return our joy in the middle of sorrows, as He did for the psalmist who wrote, "weeping may stay for the night, but rejoicing comes in the morning" (Psalm 30:5b).

I want to give an example to illustrate joy: I drove throughout Uruguay for three years, teaching T3D International to over eight hundred leaders. In the last three months, I drove past a large mental institution, solidly built. It was made of concrete and had brick walls around it, three meters high. Once I had to stop at the traffic light parallel to the mental institute. It was summertime, so I rolled down my car window. Then I heard many patrons inside the high wall chanting "thirteen, thirteen, thirteen!" My curiosity got the better of me, so I pulled into the parking lot. As I got closer to the wall, the chanting got louder. I walked a meter from the wall and saw a small hole in it. When I put my right eye to the wall to try to understand why the patrons on the other side were chanting, someone inside poked me in the eye through the hole, and everyone started chanting, "fourteen, fourteen, fourteen!"

I am hoping this story made you laugh. I have given this illustration to each of the 1,200 disciples I trained, and some are still laughing! Heartfelt laughter amid your troubles can be a form of joy. My goal is to give you a taste of this medicine.

Ecclesiastes 3:4 says that there is "a time to weep and a time to laugh, a time to mourn and a time to dance." I need to teach you about having the joy of the Lord in your life and ministry. You have had a lifetime of difficulties and simply forgotten how to laugh and how to minister in joy! Lord willing, I will write a book soon about the theology of joy! The Bible is replete with scriptures about joy.

Make a daily habit of reading in the Bible and you will see how many times the Old and New Testaments talk about joy! I will teach you a few scriptures about joy. These scriptures that I will share also demonstrate the strategy Jesus used to evangelize in new regions.

Mark 6:6-13

Then Jesus went around teaching from village to village. Calling the Twelve to him, he sent them out two by two and gave them authority over impure spirits. These were his instructions: "Take nothing for the journey except a staff—no bread, no bag, no money in your belts. Wear sandals but not an extra shirt. Whenever you enter a house, stay there until you leave that town. And if any place will not welcome you or listen to you, leave that place and shake the dust off your feet as a testimony against them." They went out and preached that people should repent. They drove out many demons and anointed many sick people with oil and healed them.

In these verses, Jesus sent out His twelve disciples ahead of himself, two by two, and gave them authority to do the work of a disciple before they left. This is an advanced formula for evangelizing on a greater scale. Plan to evangelize areas like Jesus did. In faith, ask the Lord to help you as teams of T3D International disciples to evangelize towns. You can send out graduated T3D International disciples in exactly the way you read about in Mark 6:12-13: "They went out and preached that people should repent. They drove out many demons and anointed many sick people with oil and healed them."

Combine what you learned in my teaching about the theology of salvation with this scripture. Lead T3D International disciples to new areas for the Lord. Once the people you speak to have Jesus in their hearts, begin to train them with the T3D International program.

Luke 10:1-24

After this the Lord appointed seventy-two others and sent them two by two ahead of him to every town and place where he was about to go. He told them, "The harvest is plentiful, but the workers are few. Ask the Lord of the harvest, therefore, to send out workers into his harvest field. Go! I am sending you out like lambs among wolves…. When you enter a house, first say, 'Peace to this house.' If someone who promotes peace is there, your peace will rest on them; if not, it will return to you. Stay there, eating and drinking whatever they give you, for the worker deserves his wages. Do not move around from house to house. When you enter a town and are welcomed, eat what is offered to you. Heal the sick who are there and tell them, 'The Kingdom of God has come near to you.' But when you enter a town and are not welcomed, go into its streets, and say, 'Even the dust of your town we wipe from our feet as a warning to you. Yet be sure of this: The kingdom of God has come near.'…. if the miracles that were performed in you had been performed in Tyre and Sidon, they would have repented long ago, sitting in sackcloth and ashes…. Whoever listens to you listens to me; he who rejects you rejects me; but whoever rejects me rejects him who sent me." The seventy-two returned with joy and said, "Lord, even the demons submit to us in your name." He replied, "I saw Satan fall like lightning from heaven. I have given you authority to trample on snakes and scorpions and to overcome all the power of the enemy; nothing will harm you. However, do not rejoice that the spirits submit to you, but rejoice that your names are written in heaven." At that time Jesus, full of joy through the Holy Spirit, said, "I praise you, Father, Lord of heaven and earth, because you have hidden these things from the wise and learned, and revealed them to little children. Yes, Father, for this is what you were pleased to do. All things have been committed to me by my Father. No one knows who the Son is except the Father, and no one knows who the Father is except the Son and those to whom the Son chooses to reveal him." Then he turned to his disciples and said privately, "Blessed are the eyes that see what you see. For I tell you that many prophets and kings wanted to see what you see but did not see it, and to hear what you hear but did not hear it."

I will clarify for you some specific verses from this passage in Luke 10.

Luke 10:1: The Lord appointed seventy-two others and sent them two by two ahead of Him to every town and place where He was about to go. How wise of the Lord to send out His disciples two by two! This makes you think about the ark in Genesis. The Lord sent out disciples into towns where He was going to go minister. The disciples were to prepare the people ahead of time for the Kingdom message, for when Jesus arrived.

Luke 10:2-3: He told them, "The harvest is plentiful, but the workers are few. Ask the Lord of the harvest, therefore, to send out workers into His harvest field. Go! I am sending you out like lambs among wolves." The harvest is plentiful around the world, but there are not many workers. In this scripture, we are told to ask the Lord of the harvest to send out workers. Stop reading for a moment and ask Him to send you and your new disciples to His Harvest. Pray this prayer: "Lord, please send me." I am praying that my T3D International teaching will prepare you to make disciples so we will have enough workers to reach the vast last-day harvest.

You are God's disciple! You are one of those workers now that you are a part of T3D International. You have been chosen by the Trinity to help bring in the harvest. You are the answer to your own prayer. I know that this is true because the next part of the verse says, "go!" Remember I taught during the first day of theology, the word "go" in Matthew 28:19 means "in your going?" Then Jesus says, "I am sending YOU out." Do not look to the left or right for others who you think may be better equipped than you are. Believe me, if you are reading this book, you are ready to go! He is sending you out into the harvest. He has given each of us specific talents. Ask the Lord about the talents He has given you and how He wants you to use them.

The next verses in Luke 10 deal with a more advanced topic of evangelism. For now, it is sufficient to say that we are taught how to go, how to act, and how to evangelize. We are told to say "peace" when we enter a place. Can you imagine how many evangelistic opportunities would open to us if we began to say in a loud voice, "peace!" whenever we entered a home, a business, or our own churches? These verses also teach us not to get upset when we are rejected. Rejection can produce strong emotions. Rejection at times produces fear, which causes a desire for self-preservation, and results in us ceasing to evangelize or train disciples. We need to remember that people are not rejecting us, they are rejecting the one who sent us.

Luke 10:17: The seventy-two returned with joy and said, "Lord, even the demons submit to us in your name." I love this verse. It is a core tenet of my T3D International teaching. I am sending you out as teams of one to five people to accomplish your Social/Evangelistic Project. You are being sent out with T3D International training, much like Jesus's disciples were sent out with training. A team of disciples provides protection from rejection and the ability to use individual gifts from the Holy Spirit. The Holy Spirit will use the combination of the team members' gifts to accomplish the miracles necessary for the project you are going to complete. This project will also prepare the hearts of the people for the gospel. The Social/Evangelistic Project is a kind way to evangelize, rather than forced and condemning. In my day, evangelism meant knocking on doors (and praying that the person you were supposed to witness to was not home.) In Ecuador, I taught two hundred people at a time, so I divided all the leaders into forty groups of five leaders each. They went out as teams to accomplish their Social/Evangelistic Projects. When they returned from blessing others, they were full of joy!

After you read my book, I expect you to teach a minimum of three disciples. If you do not feel ready, teach at least one. If you feel confident to teach the material of this book, you can train as many disciples at a time as you and the Lord decide. In Luke 10:1, Jesus sent his disciples out "two by two." Whether you are a team of two, four (you and three more), or five people, you will have one another for mutual encouragement and support to continue.

Everyone on the team must take part in the Social/Evangelistic Project in some way or another. The Holy Spirit pours out His anointing in a special way as you "go" and sacrificially do His will for others. Begin thinking about your Social/Evangelistic Project (see Chapter Twelve) and the creative ideas that can be produced through your talents (or your team's collective talents). Do not be concerned if you repeat one of the projects that has already been done. This is just a start for you and your disciples. It is important to start somewhere. Once you get an idea of how the project works, keep making disciples and keep creating new Social/Evangelistic Projects. You just need to complete a project before you can graduate from the T3D International course.

The key part of Luke 10:17 is that "the seventy-two returned with **joy**" (emphasis mine). The Lord gives joy to you as you do His work for others! It is hard to fathom this, but He will give you heartfelt joy as you sacrificially work for the benefit of others. Think about this: you will creatively decide how to bless someone else, you will use your own funds and time to complete the work, and the Lord will have you return with joy. Joy is not something you can buy. Joy is a heartfelt blessing that radiates from being blessed by the Holy Spirit for serving someone else. How could seventy-two disciples return with joy after the sacrifices they made to "go?" These scriptures reveal the touch of the Holy Spirit on the disciples. When you continue as a disciple, He will touch your heart, too!

Luke 10:17-20: "Lord, even the demons submit to us in your name." [Jesus] replied, "I saw Satan fall like lightning from heaven….do not rejoice that the spirits submit to you, but rejoice that your names are written in heaven." Jesus spoke these words to His disciples. You are His disciples, so these words will apply to you as you make disciples and minister to others "in your going." Jesus said that His disciples should not rejoice because spirits are subject to them, but because their names are written in heaven. Think about the joy you will receive from the Holy Spirit when you minister to others. Now magnify that joy as you remember that your name is written in heaven. Your sacrifices turn into blessings that produce immense joy.

One important part of Luke 10:21 that is often missed is the Trinity formula of joy: "At that time Jesus, full of joy through the Holy Spirit, said, 'I praise you, Father, Lord of heaven and earth.'" Joy must be important to the Trinity because this scripture interweaves joy, ministry, and the Trinity. Jesus is our example. Allow the Holy Spirit to fill your heart with His joy. My heart is filled with the joy of the Holy Spirit when I hear about the work that T3D International disciples do.

Luke 10:23: Then [Jesus] turned to his disciples and said privately, "Blessed are the eyes that see what you see." In your prayer time or as you walk with Jesus, He will say privately to you as His disciple that you are blessed by the Trinity as you see with your heart how glorious it is to accomplish His will, train disciples, and bless others. We receive spiritual benefits for obeying God and doing His will.

I would like to share a few last verses from other books of the Bible.

John 16:23-24

"In that day you will no longer ask me anything. Very truly I tell you, my Father will give you whatever you ask in my name. Until now you have not asked for anything in my name. Ask and you will receive, and your joy will be complete."

Are you sad of heart, depressed, and do not know what to do or where you are heading? Would you like to have abundant joy right now? These verses are for you. Ask your Father directly to send you into the harvest as a trained T3D International disciple. Get started now. Find other leaders and begin training them. Complete a Social/ Evangelistic Project together. The Lord will fill your heart with the abundant joy of the Trinity.

Deuteronomy 28:47-48

"Because you did not serve the LORD your God joyfully and gladly in the time of prosperity, therefore in hunger and thirst, in nakedness and dire poverty, you will serve the enemies the LORD sends against you."

We are always left with choices of life and death with the Lord. It is difficult to face the circumstances of life alone when we do not trust the Lord with His joy and enthusiasm. Check yourself and see where you are.

In Genesis I saw a question that made me wonder where each of us are today. God called out and asked Adam, "Where are you?" Are you kidding me? In a small garden, a place where God walked daily with His creation, He did not know where Adam was? Oy vey! Adam hid because of his sin, like many of us. Sin kills the joy in our lives. He made a leaf suit to "cover" his sins. God called out to Adam not because of His lack of knowledge, but because of His Omniscience (God's total knowledge of all things, always. This term will be explained in the next theology). God called out to Adam so that

Adam would think about "where he was" physically and spiritually! Adam was not in a good place in his life.

Sometimes we, too, do not know where we are. The Lord is calling out your name. Where are you? Ask the Father to forgive you. Ask Him to help you do His will. Obey Him and train disciples. Learn to walk in the joy of the Trinity as you sacrificially serve others.

Chapter Eight:
T3D International Workbook

Please fill in the blanks.

How is joy a theology, a study about God? Joy is a condition of the heart, not a momentary emotion like happiness. Happiness is situational. A cake at a birthday party can bring happiness. _____ is a permanent condition of the heart that comes from _____ in the work of God. In Nehemiah 8:10, the Israelites are told, "do not grieve, for the joy of the Lord is your _____.'" Even in difficult times, the Trinity gives us joy.

Ecclesiastes 3:4 says that there is "a time to weep and a time to laugh, a time to mourn and a time to dance." I need to teach you about having the joy of the Lord in your life and _____. You have had a lifetime of difficulties and simply forgotten how to laugh and how to in _____! The Bible is replete with scriptures about joy.

Make a _____ of reading in the Bible and you will see how many times the Old and New Testaments talk about joy! I will teach you a few scriptures about joy.

Luke 10:1-24

After this the Lord appointed seventy-two others and sent them two by two ahead of him to every town and place where he was about to go. He told them, "The _____ is _____, but the workers are _____. Ask the Lord of the harvest, therefore, to _____ out _____ into his harvest field. Go! I am sending you out like lambs among wolves.… When you enter a house, first say, 'Peace to this house.' If someone who promotes peace is there, your peace will rest on them; if not, it will return to you.…" The seventy-two returned with _____ and said, "Lord, even the demons submit to us in your name." He replied, "I saw Satan fall like lightning from heaven. I have given you authority to trample on snakes and scorpions and to overcome all the power of the enemy; nothing will harm you. However, do not rejoice that the spirits submit to you, but rejoice that your names are written in heaven." At that time _____, full of _____ through the Holy Spirit, said, "I praise you, Father, Lord of heaven and earth, because you have hidden these things from the wise and learned, and revealed them to little children. Yes, Father, for this is what you were pleased to do. All things have been committed to me by my Father. No one knows who the Son is except the Father, and no one knows who the Father is except the Son and those to whom the Son chooses to reveal him."

I will clarify for you some specific verses from this passage in Luke 10.

Luke 10:1: The Lord appointed seventy-two others and sent them two by two ahead of Him to every town and place where He was about to go. How wise of the Lord to send out _____ two by two!

Luke 10:2-3: He told them, "The harvest is plentiful, but the workers are few. Ask the Lord of the harvest, therefore, to send out workers into His harvest field. Go! I am sending you out like lambs among wolves." The _____ is _____ around the world, but there are not many workers. In this scripture, we are told to _____ the Lord of the harvest to send out _____. You are God's _____! You are one of those now that you are a part of T3D International. You have been chosen by the Trinity to help bring in the harvest. You are the _____ to your own prayer. I know that this is true because the next part of the verse says, "go!" Remember I taught during the first day of theology, the word "go" in Matthew 28:19 means "in your _____?" Then Jesus says, "I _____ am _____ YOU out." Do not look to the left or right for others who you think may be better than you are. Believe me, if you are reading this book, you are ready to go! He is sending you out into the harvest. He has _____ each of us specific talents. Ask the Lord about the _____ He has given you and how He wants you to use them.

Luke 10:17: The seventy-two returned with joy and said, "Lord, even the demons submit to us in your name." I love this verse. It is a tenet of my T3D International teaching. I am sending you out as teams of one to five people to accomplish your Social/Evangelistic Project. You are being sent out with T3D International _____, much like Jesus's disciples were sent out with training. A team of disciples provides _____ from rejection and the ability to use _____ gifts from the Holy Spirit. The _____ will use the combination of the team members' gifts to accomplish the miracles necessary for the project you are going to complete. This project will also _____ the hearts of the people for the gospel. The key part of Luke 10:17 is that "the seventy-two _____ with **joy**" (emphasis mine). The Lord gives joy to you as you do His work for others! It is hard to fathom this, but He will give you heartfelt joy as you _____ work for the benefit of others. Think about this: you will creatively decide how to bless someone else, you will use your own funds and time to complete the work, and the Lord will have you return with joy. _____ is not something you can buy. Joy is a heartfelt blessing that radiates from being blessed by the Holy Spirit for serving someone else. How could seventy-two disciples with _____ after the sacrifices they made to "go?" These scriptures reveal the _____ of the Holy Spirit on the disciples. When you continue as a disciple, He will touch your heart, too! One important part of Luke 10:21 that is often missed is the Trinity formula of joy: "At that time Jesus, _____ of ____ through the Holy , said, 'I praise you, Father, Lord of heaven and earth.'" Joy must be _____ to the _____ because this scripture interweaves joy, ministry, and the Trinity. Jesus is our example. _____the Holy Spirit to fill your heart with His joy. My heart is filled with the joy of the Holy Spirit when I hear about the work that T3D International disciples do.

Luke 10:23: Then [Jesus] turned to his disciples and said privately, "Blessed are the eyes that see what you see." In your prayer time or as you walk with Jesus, He will say privately to you as His disciple that you are blessed by the Trinity as you see with your heart how glorious it is to accomplish His will, train disciples, and bless others. We receive spiritual benefits for obeying God and doing His will.

Chapter Nine:
Theology of Three Characteristics of God

The three characteristics of God are considered systematic theology. I will teach you by giving you scriptural references about each of the three characteristics: omniscience, omnipotence, and omnipresence. The entire Bible reveals these three characteristics.

One of the characteristics attributed to the Trinity is omniscience, the quality of being all-knowing. This means God knows everything in the past, present, and future. Here are some Old and New Testament references to ponder.

Job 21:22: "Can anyone teach knowledge to God, since he judges even the highest?" Can a three-year-old teach you quantum physics? Some say that we function using only ten percent of our brains. God's knowledge is above all humans.

Psalm 147:4: [The Lord] determines the number of the stars and calls them each by name. Take a moment tonight to peek at the stars. Humans cannot even see all the stars using our most powerful telescopes. God is relational. He took time to number and name the stars individually.

Psalm 147:5: Great is our Lord and mighty in power; his understanding has no limit. Humans have many limits; God has none. We need to learn to be more like Him. Take on the mind of Christ. We must abide in Him so we can be more like Him each day. Being like Christ every day means being discipled by the Triune God.

Jeremiah 1:5: "Before I formed you in the womb, I knew you." God's omniscience includes knowledge of every human ever born. The Bible declares to us that God knew us in the womb. This is one of two scriptures that allows me to make my T3D International assertion that each of us is an original. I believe Jeremiah 1:5 describes the precise moment of formation when God individually signed us with fingerprints and toe prints before we were born. Nobody was born before us, or will be born after us, who has that exact print; our prints will never be duplicated.

Now think about this: God signs everyone, even in the Old Testament before Jesus. The Bible says that He knew Moses by name. I am sure he had fingerprints. Psalm 139:15 says, "You watched me as I was being formed in utter seclusion, as I was woven together in the dark of the womb" (NLT). You are an original. If you are original, you are not just anyone. God believes in you. You are worth a lot to the relational God. Honor Him with your life. Make disciples who honor Him. You may not be aware of those that you will rescue as you train.

Matthew 6:8: "Do not be like them; for your Father knows what you need before you ask Him." Before you can even speak, God knows your needs. It does not matter what culture you are from or whether you are young or old, rich or poor, and male or female. He is a relational God who loves and cares for you. Because the Trinity is omniscient, you are never alone; you have been known and loved before even time was created.

Luke 12:7: "Indeed, the very hairs of your head are all numbered. Don't be afraid; you are worth more than many sparrows." Try to count the number of hairs on your head. It is impossible, right? Yet God has a constant running count. He is a God who desires a personal relationship with each of us. Only an all-knowing God could proclaim that He knows you to the core of your DNA.

1 Corinthians 2:11: No one knows the thoughts of God except the Spirit of God. Only the Trinity understands the Trinity. In other words, no human can know God. Not even the devil can know God—if he had been omniscient, he would never have worked so hard to crucify Jesus. Jesus's sacrifice destroyed the enemy and freed those who accept the resurrected Jesus.

Hebrews 4:13: Nothing in all creation is hidden from God's sight. Everything is uncovered and laid bare before the eyes of him to whom we must give account. Remember in Genesis when Adam tried to hide from God behind a suit of leaves? That did not work in Genesis, and it will not work now, however you try to hide. Be bold and come to Him in truthfulness. Tell God that you have sinned against Him and allow Him to forgive you. God's omniscience means that He sees all our sin and we cannot hide from Him. The Trinity never wants us to hide like Adam in the garden; He always wants us to run to Him.

Another characteristic of God is his omnipotence. This means that all power is attributed to Him, and he is capable of doing whatever He wants.

Genesis 18:14: "Is anything too hard for the Lord?" God gave a baby to Sarah and Abraham when they were advanced in age. Impossible! Likewise, in Matthew 1:18, "[Mary] was found to be pregnant through the Holy Spirit." The Lord gave a virgin girl a child named Jesus. Impossible! Yet God is all-powerful and loves to do the impossible.

Psalm 115:3: Our God is in heaven; he does whatever pleases him. Only an all-powerful God can do what He pleases. Many times, we do not understand what He is doing. Learn to trust Him. He is faithful and knows the plans He has for you.

Isaiah 55:11: "...so is my word that goes out from my mouth: It will not return to me empty, but will accomplish what I desire and achieve the purpose for which I sent it." Every word that God has spoken and will speak through His Word will accomplish His desires. In

Genesis He spoke creation into existence; He can speak life into your world right now. Believe Him! Genesis is the book of beginnings. We can still see the creation principles we read in Genesis in our world today. If you are having a difficult time right now, go look at a tree near you and think about how God created trees back in Genesis. He is so powerful that we still experience the things He created. Use faith to believe Him in your tough moments. Do you need an all-powerful God in your life right now? He is only a breath away from you.

Jeremiah 32:17: "Ah, Sovereign Lord, you have made the heavens and the earth by your great power and outstretched arm. Nothing is too hard for You." Something may be hard for you, but there is nothing too hard for God. Muse on His power and His relationship with you. He wants to bless you as you begin to train T3D International disciples.

Matthew 19:26: Jesus looked at them and said, "With man this is impossible, but with God all things are possible." I believe that the word "impossible" is one of God's favorite words. Place the impossible on your Father's shoulders. He cares for you.

Luke 12:7: "Indeed, the very hairs of your head are all numbered. Don't be afraid; you are worth more than many sparrows." Have you ever heard a sparrow walking up and down a branch, saying, "how am I going to eat today?" How many sparrows are there in the entire world? God feeds them all. Do not worry; He can provide for your basic needs. Do not let the sparrow catch you worrying. Do not make the sparrow wonder, "Don't these humans know that God provides?"

John 3:16-17: For God so loved the world that he gave his one and only Son, that whoever believes in Him shall not perish but have eternal life. For God did not send his Son into the world to condemn the world, but to save the world through him. Only an all-powerful God can snatch you from the fire and give you eternal life. Only an all-powerful God can give you His only son. This is a core Bible verse about God's powerful love and personal sacrifice for His creation. The entire Bible is about our relational God and His creation.

Romans 1:20: For since the creation of the world God's invisible qualities—his eternal power and divine nature—have been clearly seen, being understood from what has been made, so that people are without excuse. God's invisible qualities are not thought about much, but the invisible is more important than the visible. Remember, even before the creation of the world, when nothing else existed, the Trinity existed. Disciples need to learn how to spend more time understanding the invisible things of God. This scripture talks about how the eternal powers of our invisible God are clearly seen. We just need to stand at the foot of Victoria Falls in Africa, to feel the power of the God who created the world.

Romans 15:18-19: I will not venture to speak of anything except what Christ has accomplished through me in leading the Gentiles to obey God by what I have said and done—by the power of signs and wonders, through the power of the Spirit of God. You can find the Trinity in these scriptures. As you read the Bible, keep track of how many times the Trinity is mentioned from Genesis to Revelation. God's omnipotence is seen through the signs and wonders that Christ allows Paul to perform as he ministers to the Gentiles.

Ephesians 1:17, 19-20: I keep asking that the God of our Lord Jesus Christ, the glorious Father, may give you the Spirit of wisdom and revelation, so that you may know him better....[and] his incomparably great power for us who believe. That power is the same as the mighty strength he exerted when he raised Christ from the dead. There are marvelous verses to muse on in Ephesians. The power God gives you is the same strength He used to raise Jesus from the dead. He gives us all of who He is. We need to learn to know Him more. T3D International is about learning how to know God. The verses from Ephesians may seem to say more about God's omniscience than His omnipotence. However, I want to focus on the idea of how much power was needed to raise Jesus from the dead. God has that power and more.

We will now move to the third characteristic. Omnipresence is the Trinity's ability to be present everywhere at the same time. This means that the Trinity's knowledge and power are also everywhere at the same time.

Psalm 33:13-14: From heaven the Lord looks down and sees all mankind; from his dwelling place he watches all who live on earth.

Psalm 46:1: God is our refuge and strength, an ever-present help in trouble. These two verses speak about a relational God who sees all of humankind and is ready to help when we are in need. Part of learning about God is learning that He is always with us. The thought of God being everywhere is too weighty for me to comprehend. There are approximately eight billion people living in the world. God knows them all intimately. He knows the universe from the simplest cell to the emptiness on the other side of the stars. Yet He knows your intimate needs as an individual and cares enough to save your every tear.

Psalm 139:7-8: Where can I go from your Spirit? Where can I flee from Your presence? If I go up to the heavens, you are there; if I make my bed in the depths, you are there. You can never escape God's presence no matter how far you run and hide—ask Adam. Proverbs 15:3 says that "the eyes of the Lord are everywhere, keeping watch on the wicked and the good." This verse shows that our God is everywhere. He watches everyone, good and evil. Where can we go to escape our God? The inference is that we can never escape Him.

Jeremiah 1:5: "Before I formed you in the womb I knew you, before you were born I set you apart." I believe that God has formed and known every child, and is in every womb that has ever carried a child. Talk about omnipresence! It is not a far jump for me to say that He signed us all with original fingerprints!

In these next verses, all three of God's characteristics are present. Look at each verse. Try to identify the three characteristics in each passage before reading the explanation.

John 4:46-53:

And there was a certain royal official whose son lay sick at Capernaum. When this man heard that Jesus had arrived in Galilee from Judea, he went to him and begged him to come and heal his son, who was close to death. "Unless you people see signs and wonders," Jesus told him, "you will never believe." The royal official said, "Sir, come down before my child dies." "Go," Jesus replied, "your son will live." The man took Jesus at his word and departed. While he was still on the way, his servants met him with the news that his boy was living. When he inquired as to the time when his son got better, they said to him, "Yesterday, at one in the afternoon, the fever left him." Then the father realized that this was the exact time at which Jesus had said to him, "Your son will live." So he his whole household believed.

All three characteristics of God are visible in John 4:50: "'Go' Jesus replied, 'your son will live.' The man took Jesus at his word and departed." God's omniscience was demonstrated as He told the man that His child would live. His omnipotence was in the healing. He took the son from death to life, just as He does for us as we believe in Him. His omnipresence was demonstrated when He was speaking to the father and at the same time was with the son. Try to see these characteristics as you read God's Word.

Hebrews 13:8:

Jesus Christ is the same yesterday and today and forever.

Psalm 90:12:

Teach us to number our days, that we may gain a heart of wisdom.

When I calculate my life to eighty years of age, I have 780 weekends left. How many weekends would you have if you calculated a lifespan of eighty years? The Bible exhorts us to "count our days." These types of thoughts help your eschatology. Eschatology is the study of the "end day things." Biblical eschatology is a part of systematic theology; it studies the prophecies that speak about the events that human beings will experience in the last days of history. We will be more careful if we know that our days are numbered. The knowledge that our days are limited will change what we do now. Ask a Christian the question, "What would you do now if you knew that Jesus was going to return next Wednesday?" This is an eschatological question. The answer is, "I would do nothing different!" If a Christian says, "I would disciple more people," "I would win more people to Jesus," or "I would read my Bible more," their eschatology demands that they should be doing these things now. If they were, there would be no need for change.

I hope you can see the importance of this study for you and the disciples you will train. I have been seeing the Lord this closely in my reading of His Word, cover to cover, over forty-seven times. He invites you closer. Sometimes He will say "go" and sometimes He says "come." Is He saying "come" to you now? He said that to Peter. Peter said, "Lord, if it's you…tell me to come to you" (Matthew 14:28). Peter started to walk by faith on the word "come!" I invite you to apply these scriptures and come to the Father. Pray by faith. Come to Him today and obey Him.

Chapter Nine:
T3D International Workbook

Please fill in the blanks.

The three _____ of God are considered _____ theology. I will teach you by giving you scriptural references about each of the three characteristics: omniscience, omnipotence, and omnipresence. The entire Bible reveals these three characteristics. One of the characteristics attributed to the Trinity is _____, the quality of being all-knowing. This means God knows everything in the past, present, and future. Here are some Old and New Testament references to ponder.

Job 21:22: "Can anyone teach knowledge to God, since he judges even the highest?" Can a three-year-old teach you quantum physics? Some say that we function using only ten percent of our brains. God's _____ is above all humans.

Psalm 147:4: [The Lord] determines the number of the stars and calls them each by name. Take a moment tonight to peek at the stars. Humans cannot even see all the stars using our most powerful _____. God is relational. He took time to _____ and name the stars individually.

Psalm 147:5: Great is our Lord and mighty in _____; his understanding has no limit. Humans have many limits; God has none. We need to learn to be more like Him. Take on the mind of

Christ. We must _____ in Him so we can be more like Him each day. Being like Christ every day means being discipled by the Triune God.

Jeremiah 1:5: "Before I _____ you in the womb, I knew you." God's omniscience includes knowledge of _____ ever born. The Bible declares to us that God knew us in the womb. This is one of two scriptures that allows me to make my T3D International assertion that each of us is an _____. I believe Jeremiah 1:5 describes the precise moment of formation when God individually signed us with _____ and toe prints before we were born. Nobody was born before us, or will be born after us, who has that exact print; our prints will never be duplicated.

Matthew 6:8: "Do not be like them; for your Father _____ what you need before you ask Him." Before you can even _____, God knows your needs. It does not matter what _____ you are from or whether you are young or old, rich or poor, and male or female. He is a _____ God who loves and cares for you. Because the Trinity is omniscient, you are never alone; you have been known and loved before even time was created.

Luke 12:7: "Indeed, the very hairs of your head are all _____. Don't be afraid; you are worth more than many sparrows." Try to count the number of _____ on your head. It is impossible, right? Yet God has a constant running count. He is a God who desires a personal relationship with each of us. Only an all-knowing God could proclaim that He knows you to the core of your DNA.

Hebrews 4:13: Nothing in all creation is hidden from God's sight. Everything is uncovered and laid bare before the eyes of him to whom we must give account. Remember in Genesis when Adam tried to from _____ behind a suit of leaves? That did not work in Genesis, and it will not work now, however you try to hide. Be bold and come to Him in _____. Tell God that you have sinned against Him and allow Him to forgive you. God's omniscience means that He sees all our sin and we cannot hide from Him. The Trinity never wants us to hide like Adam in the garden; He always wants us to run to Him.

Another characteristic of God is his omnipotence. This means that all power is attributed to Him, and he is capable of doing whatever He wants.

Genesis 18:14: "Is anything too_____ for the Lord?" God gave a baby to Sarah and Abraham when they were advanced in age. Impossible! Likewise, in Matthew 1:18, "[Mary] was found to be _____ through the Holy Spirit." The Lord gave a _____ girl a child named Jesus. Impossible! Yet God is all-powerful and loves to do the impossible.

Psalm 115:3: Our God is in heaven; he does whatever pleases him. Only an_____ God can do what He pleases. Many times, we do not understand what He is doing. Learn to trust Him. He is faithful and _____ the _____ He has for you.

Isaiah 55:11: "...so is my word that goes out from my mouth: It will not return to me empty, but will accomplish what I _____ *and* _____ *the purpose for which I sent it."* Every word that God has spoken and will speak through His Word will accomplish His desires. In Genesis He spoke creation into existence; He can speak life into your world right now. Believe Him! Genesis is the book of _____ . We can still see the creation principles we read in Genesis in our world today. If you are having a difficult time right now, go look at a tree near you and think about how w _____ trees back in Genesis. He is so powerful that we still experience the things He created. Use faith to believe Him in your tough moments. Do you need an all-powerful God in your life right now? He is only a breath away from you.

Jeremiah 32:17: "Ah, Sovereign Lord, you have made the heavens and the earth by your great power and outstretched arm. Nothing is too hard for You." Something may be hard for you, but there is too _____ for God. Muse on His power and His relationship with you. He wants to bless you as you begin to train T3D International disciples.

Matthew 19:26: Jesus looked at them and said, "With man this is _____ *, but with God all things are possible."* I believe that the word "impossible" is one of God's favorite words. Place the impossible on your Father's shoulders. He cares for you.

John 3:16-17: For God so loved the world that he gave his one and only Son, that whoever believes in Him shall not _____ *but have eternal life.* For God did not send his Son into the world to condemn the world, but to save the world through him. Only an all-powerful God can snatch you from the fire and give you eternal life. Only an all-powerful God can _____ you His only son. This is a core Bible verse about God's powerful love and personal sacrifice for His creation. The entire Bible is about our relational God and His creation.

Romans 1:20: For since the creation of the world God's invisible qualities—his eternal _____ and divine nature—have been clearly seen, being understood from what has been made, so that people are without excuse. God's _____ qualities are not thought about much, but the invisible is more important than the visible. Remember, even before the _____ of the world, when nothing else existed, the Trinity existed. Disciples need to learn how to spend more time understanding the invisible things of God. This scripture talks about how the eternal powers of our invisible God are clearly seen. We just need to stand at the foot of Victoria Falls in Africa, to feel the power of the God who created the world.

Ephesians 1:17, 19-20, "I keep asking that the God of our Lord Jesus Christ, the glorious Father, may give you the Spirit of wisdom and revelation, so that you may know him better….[and] his incomparably great power for us who believe. That power is the same as the mighty strength he exerted when he raised Christ from the dead. There are marvelous verses to muse on in Ephesians. The power God gives you is the same strength He used to _____ Jesus from the dead. He gives us all of who He is. We need to learn to know Him more. T3D International is about learning how to know God. The verses from Ephesians may seem to say more about God's omniscience than His omnipotence. However, I want to focus on the idea of how much _____ was _____ to raise Jesus from the dead. God has that power and more.

We will now move to the third characteristic. _____ is the Trinity's ability to be _____ at the same time. This means that the Trinity's knowledge and power are also everywhere at the same time.

Psalm 33:13-14: From heaven the Lord looks down and _____ *all* _____ *; from his dwelling place he watches all who live on earth.*

Psalm 46:1: God is our refuge and strength, an _____ *help in trouble.* These two verses speak about a relational God who sees all of humankind and is _____ to _____ when we are in need. Part of _____ about God is learning that He is always with us. The thought of God being _____ is too weighty for me to comprehend. There are approximately eight billion people living in the world. God knows them all intimately. He knows the universe from the simplest cell to the emptiness on the other side of the stars. Yet He _____ your _____ needs as an individual and cares enough to save your every tear.

Psalm 139:7-8: Where can I go from your Spirit? Where can I flee from Your presence? If I go up to the heavens, you are there; if I make my bed in the depths, you are there. You can never escape God's _____ no matter how far you run and hide—ask Adam.

Proverbs 15:3 says that "the eyes of the Lord are _____, keeping watch on the wicked and the good." This verse shows that our God is everywhere. He watches _____, good and evil. Where can we go to escape our God? The inference is that we can never escape Him.

Jeremiah 1:5: "Before I formed you in the womb I knew you, before you were born I set you apart." I believe that God has formed and known every child, and is in every womb that has ever carried a child. Talk about omnipresence! It is not a far jump for me to say that He signed us all with original fingerprints!

In these next verses, all three of God's characteristics are present. Look at each verse. Try to identify the three characteristics in each passage before reading the explanation.

John 4:46-53:

And there was a certain royal official whose son lay sick at Capernaum. When this man heard that Jesus had arrived in Galilee from Judea, he went to him and begged him to come and heal his son, who was close to death. "Unless you people see signs and wonders," Jesus told him, "you will never believe." The royal official said, "Sir, come down before my child dies." "Go," Jesus replied, "your son will live." The man took Jesus at his word and departed. While he was still on the way, his servants met him with the news that his boy was living. When he inquired as to the time when his son got better, they said to him, "Yesterday, at one in the afternoon, the fever left him." Then the father realized that this was the exact time at which Jesus had said to him, "Your son will live." So he his whole household believed.

All three characteristics of God are visible in John 4:50: "'Go' Jesus replied, 'your son will live.' The man took Jesus at his word and departed." God's _____ was demonstrated as He told the man that His child would live. His _____ was in the healing. He took the son from death to life, just as He does for us as we believe in Him. His _____ was demonstrated when He was speaking to the father and at the same time was with the son. Try to see these characteristics as you read God's Word.

Chapter Ten:
Theology of Jesus Praying

How is Jesus praying a theology? When you take time to pray for someone, you are showing kindness. You care about that person. You are asking for God's divine intervention. The fact that Jesus prayed identifies Him as a loving part of the Trinity. He is praying to His Father specifically for His own twelve disciples who will be making other disciples. We can identify with His prayer as we study T3D International. The teaching of this theology is focused on the core of Jesus's private prayers to His Father. Jesus is prayed for His current disciples and every disciple since; His prayers affect you today! Jesus's personal and private prayer reveals a theology about an omnipotent, caring, and relational God.

I am going to focus specifically on Jesus's private prayer to His Father in John 17, and give extra attention to certain verses. Would it be worth it to you to listen to a private prayer that Jesus prayed two thousand years ago?

Look at the definitions for the words "relative" and "relevant." "Relative" means having a connection to or dependency on something else. "Relevant" means something is pertinent and applicable to your circumstances. Jesus's prayers in John 17 incorporate these definitions, and you should keep them in mind as you study this scripture. You are connected to and have a dependency on His prayers, and the Bible is relevant to all cultures throughout time. Jesus's prayer is just as pertinent to you today as when He prayed privately to His Father in John 17.

I am going to teach you how much Jesus cares about you. You are going to be a fly on the wall, listening as Jesus made a private prayer to his Father two millennia ago. You are so important to the Lord that His prayers are as relevant, impactful, and applicable to you as they were to His own disciples. Let us break down His prayer.

John 17:1-5

[Jesus] looked toward heaven and prayed: "Father, the hour has come. Glorify your Son, that your Son may glorify you. For you granted him authority over all people that he might give eternal life to all those you have given him. Now this is eternal life: that they know you, the only true God, and Jesus Christ, whom you have sent. I have brought you glory on earth by finishing the work you gave me to do. And now, Father, glorify me in your presence with the *glory I had with you before the world began.*"

You can see that God has given authority over all people to Jesus so He can give eternal life to all those the Father has given to Him. Jesus says eternal life means that people will know the Trinity. Jesus finished the work His Father gave Him to complete. God is at work in the world right now. How are you doing with the work that He gave you to complete? The fact that you have read my book this far signifies that you want to do the work of God. We are here at the finish of Jesus's work. Let us look at the beginning of the work He has for you: making disciples.

In the following pages, I want to address Jesus's words in John 17:5: *"And now, Father, glorify me in your presence with the glory I had with you before the world began"* (emphasis mine). I also want to mention the first thing that I believe God created, and finally look at the Trinity by means of the sixty-thousand-dollar theological word that I promised you: perichoresis.

What I believe God created first is found in Genesis 1:1: "In the beginning God created the heavens and the earth." The first thing God created was *time*: "In the beginning." Time was created for God's creation. The Trinity has no time constraints. As His creation, we are limited by time. We must respect time and use it with wisdom. I like to think about our heavenly Father standing on the platform of time, drawing back His bow and releasing His sharp arrow of love throughout the history of the Old and New Testaments, until it is driven deep into the cross of Calvary like those sharp nails that pierced His own skin!

The Father, Spirit and Son are one. We serve a relational Trinity. Let us explore the first instance where the Trinity formula is found in the Bible. It was my thought that the first Trinity formula is in Genesis 1:26: "Then God said, 'Let us make mankind in our image, in our likeness.'" The plural "us" obviously signifies more than one. Many theologians view the word "us" as a version of the Trinity formula. It is appropriate that the formula for the Trinity is found in Genesis. Most important Bible doctrines and events have roots in Genesis, the beginning. I thought that Genesis 1:26 was the first evidence of the Trinity formula—until the Spirit impressed an earlier verse on me.

Perhaps the Trinity formula is evident sooner than Genesis 1:26. Let's think about Genesis 1:1-2: "In the beginning God created the heavens and the earth. Now the earth was formless and empty, darkness was over the surface of the deep, and the Spirit of God was hovering over the waters." The very first two verses of the Bible have the Trinity formula. You see God and the Spirit, but where is Jesus? Consider John 1:1-2: "In the beginning was the Word, and the Word was with God, and the Word was God. He was with God in the beginning." It is no wonder that Jesus prayed in John 17:5, "Father, glorify me in your presence with the glory I had with you before the world began." I believe that the Trinity formula is a combination of Genesis 1:1-2 and John 1:1-2. Both scriptures begin with the phrase "in the beginning." Jesus prayed that He would be returned to the glory of the perichoresis of God.

Perichoresis is a sixty-thousand-dollar theological term that I learned as I competed my doctoral work. **Perichoresis refers to the relationship between the three persons of the triune God (Father, Son, and Holy Spirit) and the dance between them in heaven before time was created. The Trinity invites you to experience this dance with them today. Take some private time and dance in adoration with the Trinity. Jesus mentioned perichoresis in His prayer.**

We as humans cannot articulate **perichoresis or** the definition of the Trinity adequately. Our best attempts at explanation will always break down. If we use a metallurgical illustration, the Trinity would be like three super-heated kinds of liquid gold that, once combined, could no longer be distinguished separately. Perichoresis is the heavenly dance between the three members of the Trinity combined in worship. Still using a metallurgical illustration, a human, using an intense fire, would be able to distinguish between molten gold and molten iron. If we get caught up in the intense flames of the Trinity's worship, we would be able to distinguish between the divine Trinity and earthly creation. The Trinity and humans are not the same.

We know that the Trinity is not really represented in gold. This is merely my feeble attempt to illustrate how the Trinity is inviting us to the holy worship that is happening in heaven now, just like it was happening before time was created. Jesus is asking His Father to return to that glory. The Trinity invites us to be caught up in their fire.

The next set of verses portrays Jesus preparing to return home. Jesus prays that His disciples would have unity, protection, and a full measure of joy while they are still in the world. Remember that this private prayer from two thousand years ago has significance for you. I pray these same prayers for you. You can use John 17 to learn to pray for your disciples like Jesus did. If you want, read the entire chapter out loud and insert your disciples' names where it is appropriate.

John 17:11-13

"I will remain in the world no longer, but they are still in the world, and I am coming to you. Holy Father, protect them by the power of your name, the name you gave me, so that they may be one as we are one. While I was with them, I protected them and kept them safe by that name you gave me. None has been lost except the one doomed to destruction so that Scripture would be fulfilled. I am coming to you now, but I say these things while I am still in the world, so that they may have the full measure of my joy within them."

John 17:11-12: "I will remain in the world no longer, but they are still in the world, and I am coming to you. Holy Father, protect them by the power of your name." After Jesus completes His mission, He will no longer be in this world as a human. He will return to join the glory of the Trinity.

John 17:12: "While I was with them, I protected them and kept them safe…None has been lost except the one doomed to destruction so that Scripture would be fulfilled." Jesus's prayer continues to confirm His love for His disciples. His petition is for their protection. He is resolute in affirming that He "kept them safe" and lost none of them except one. When Jesus used the word "lost," it probably had the meaning that none of his disciples had been harmed. But if it meant that none of them quit, Jesus prayed that you would not quit! Take a moment to stop and pray. Ask God for the strength that the Trinity wants you to have to go forward. Jesus's prayers have immediate fulfillment in John 18. I will dedicate the next chapter to connecting John 17 and 18.

John 17:13: "I am coming to you now, but I say these things while I am still in the world, so that they may have the full measure of my joy within them." Jesus is anticipating His return, but He is praying for His disciples while He still is with them in the world. Why? So that they can continue with a "full measure of [His] joy within them." Jesus's prayer is my goal for you today as a T3D International disciple. I gave you a chapter about the theology of joy. The Trinity has linked discipleship and ministry with His joy. Do not forget you read in Luke 10:21: "Jesus, full of joy through the Holy Spirit." Joy is woven into the fabric that binds the Trinity and the disciples together.

I am not quite sure what the "full measure" Jesus speaks of denotes. But I am sure that it is not a half measure! What is the Trinity saying to His disciples today and in the future? We must have His joy to do the work of a T3D International disciple. What a powerful private prayer!

John 17:20: "My prayer is not for them alone. I pray also for those who will believe in me through their message." Jesus prayed for His existing disciples and for all their future disciples. The Trinity saw all the way into the future and prompted your heart to use this program to train others. As you study and teach the T3D International discipleship program, think about this two-thousand-year-old prayer.

I merely want you to recognize that the Trinity existed before the creation of the world, full of love in perichoresis. Jesus invites us to join this perichoresis in John 17:24: "Father, I want those you have given me to be with me where I am, and to see my glory, the glory you have given me because you loved me before the creation of the world." You will see His glory as you obey Matthew 28:19.

I want to conclude this chapter about Jesus's private prayer with this thought: I believe that we are all descendants of Jesus's trained disciples and everyone they trained. What if Peter had decided to go back to being a fisherman (which almost happened)? If one of the disciples decided not to make disciples, and they were a part of your discipleship lineage, where would you be today? Now let's extrapolate that thought. What if you decide today not to make a disciple who is trained to make other disciples?

Chapter Ten:
T3D International Workbook

Please fill in the blanks.

How is Jesus praying a theology? When you take time to pray for someone, you are _____ _____. You care about that person. You are asking for God's divine intervention. The fact that Jesus prayed identifies Him as a loving part of the Trinity. He is _____ to His Father specifically for His own twelve disciples who will be making other disciples. We can identify with His prayer as we study T3D International. The teaching of this theology is focused on the core of Jesus's _____ prayers to His Father. Jesus is prayed for His current disciples and every disciple since; His prayers affect you today! Jesus's personal and private prayer reveals a theology about an omnipotent, caring, and relational God.

I am going to focus specifically on Jesus's private prayer to His Father in John 17, and give extra attention to certain verses. Would it be worth it to you to listen to a private prayer that Jesus prayed two thousand years ago?

John 17:1-5

[Jesus] looked toward heaven and prayed: "Father, the hour has come. _____ your Son, that your Son may glorify you. For you granted him _____ over all people that he might give eternal life to all those you have given him. Now this is eternal life: that they know you, the only true God, and Jesus Christ, whom you have

_____. I have brought you glory on earth by finishing the work you gave me to do. And now, Father, glorify me in your _____ with the glory I had with you before the world began."

You can see that God has given authority over all people to Jesus so He can give eternal life to all those the Father has given to Him. Jesus says _____ _____ means that people will _____ the Trinity. Jesus finished the work His Father gave Him to complete. God is at work in the world right now. How are you doing with the work that He gave you to complete? The fact that you have read my book this far signifies that you want to do the work of God. We are here at the finish of Jesus's work. Let us look at the beginning of the work He has for you: making disciples.

In the following pages, I want to address Jesus's words in John 17:5: "And now, Father, glorify me in your presence with the glory *I had with you* _____ *the world began*" (emphasis mine). I also want to mention the first thing that I believe God created, and finally look at the Trinity by means of the sixty-thousand-dollar theological word that I promised you: perichoresis.

What I believe God created first is found in Genesis 1:1: "In the God created the heavens and the earth." The first thing God created was _____: "In the beginning." Time was created for God's creation. The Trinity has no time constraints. As His creation, we are limited by time. We must respect time and use it with wisdom.

The Father, Spirit and Son are one. We serve a relational Trinity. Let us explore the first instance where the _____ is found in the Bible. It was my thought that the first Trinity formula is in Genesis 1:26: "Then God said, 'Let us make mankind in our image, in our likeness.'" The plural "_____" obviously signifies more than one. Many theologians view the word "us" as a version of the Trinity formula. It is appropriate that the formula for the Trinity is found in Genesis. Most important Bible doctrines and events have roots in _____, the beginning. I thought that Genesis 1:26 was the first evidence of the Trinity formula—until the Spirit impressed an earlier verse on me.

Perhaps the Trinity formula is evident sooner than Genesis 1:26. Let's think about Genesis 1:1-2: "In the beginning God created the heavens and the earth. Now the earth was formless and empty, darkness was over the surface of the deep, and the _____ of God was hovering over the waters." The very first two verses of the Bible have the Trinity formula. You see _____ and the _____, but where is _____? Consider John _____: "In the beginning was the Word, and the Word was with God, and the Word was God. He was with God in the beginning." It is no wonder that Jesus prayed in John 17:5, "Father, glorify me in your presence with the glory I had with you _____ the world began." I believe that the Trinity formula is a combination of Genesis 1:1-2 and John 1:1-2. Both scriptures begin with the phrase "in the beginning." Jesus prayed that He would be returned to the glory of the _____ of God.

The next set of verses portrays Jesus preparing to _____. Jesus prays that His disciples would have unity, _____, and a full of _____ while they are still in the world. Remember that this private prayer from two thousand years ago has significance for you. I pray these same prayers for you. You can use John 17 to learn to pray for your disciples like Jesus did. If you want, read the entire chapter out loud and insert your disciples' names where it is appropriate.

John 17:11-13

"I will remain in the world no longer, but they are still in the world, and I am coming to you. Holy Father, protect them by the power of your name, the name you gave me, so that they may be one as we are one. While I was with them, I _____ them and kept them safe by that name you gave me. None has been _____ except the one to destruction so that Scripture would be fulfilled. I am coming to you now, but I say these things while I am still in the world, so that they may have the _____ measure of my ____ within them."

John 17:11-12: "I will remain in the world no longer, but they are still in the world, and I am coming to you. Holy Father, protect them by the power of your name." After Jesus completes His mission, He will no longer be in this world as a human. He will return to join the glory of the Trinity.

John 17:12: "While I was with them, I protected them and kept them safe…None has been lost except the one doomed to destruction so that Scripture would be fulfilled." Jesus's prayer continues to _____ His love for His disciples. His is for their protection. He is resolute in affirming that He "kept them safe" and lost none of them except one. When Jesus used the word "lost," it probably had the meaning that none of his disciples had been harmed. But if it meant that none of them _____, Jesus prayed that you would not quit! Take a moment to stop and _____. Ask God for the strength that the Trinity wants you to have to go forward. Jesus's prayers have immediate fulfillment in _____. I will dedicate the next chapter to connecting John 17 and 18.

John 17:13: "I am coming to you now, but I say these things while I am still in the world, so that they may have the full measure of my joy within them." Jesus is anticipating His return, but He is praying for His disciples while He still is with them in the world. Why? So that they can continue with a "full measure of [His] joy within them." Jesus's prayer is my goal for you today as a T3D International disciple. I gave you a chapter about the theology of joy. The Trinity has linked discipleship and ministry with His joy. Do not forget you read in Luke 10:21: "Jesus, full of joy through the Holy Spirit." Joy is woven into the fabric that binds the Trinity and the disciples together.

I am not quite sure what the "full measure" Jesus speaks of denotes. But I am sure that it is not a _____ measure! What is the Trinity saying to His disciples today and in the future? We must have His joy to do the work of a T3D International disciple. What a powerful _____!

John 17:20: "My prayer is not for them alone. I pray also for those who will believe in me through their message." Jesus prayed for His existing _____ and for all their future disciples. The Trinity saw all the way into the future and _____ your heart to use this program to train others. As you study and teach the T3D International discipleship program, think about this two-thousand-year-old prayer.

Chapter Eleven:
Theology of I Am

I want you to apply what you have learned and see what theology you observe as you read John 18:1-12. What can you learn about who God is and what He wants from this chapter? I am going to explore some of the verses in John 18 and expound on some theologies that I find in verses 1-12.

John 18:1-12

When he had finished praying, Jesus left with his disciples and crossed the Kidron Valley. On the other side there was a garden, and he and his disciples went into it. Now Judas, who betrayed him, knew the place, because Jesus had often met there with his disciples. So Judas came to the garden, guiding a detachment of soldiers and some officials from the chief priests and the Pharisees. They were carrying torches, lanterns, and weapons. Jesus, knowing all that was going to happen to him, went out and asked them, "Who is it you want?" "Jesus of Nazareth," they replied. "I am he," Jesus said. (And Judas the traitor was standing there with them.) When Jesus said, "I am he," they drew back and fell to the ground. Again, he asked them, "Who is it you want?" "Jesus of Nazareth," they said. Jesus answered, "I told you that I am he. If you are looking for me, then let these men go." This happened so that the words he had spoken would be fulfilled: "I have not lost one of those you gave me." Then Simon Peter, who had a sword, drew it, and struck the high priest's servant, cutting off his right ear. (The servant's name was Malchus.) Jesus commanded Peter, "Put your sword away! Shall I not drink the cup the Father has given me?" Then the detachment of soldiers with its commander and the Jewish officials arrested Jesus.

John 18:1: When he had finished praying. When you read that, your question should have been, "what did He pray about?" Read the Bible with a thirst to know what the Lord has to say. Take a quick peek at John 17:9, 11-12, 15, and 20 once again. You are the future disciples Jesus mentions in this prayer. The Trinity loves you.

In John 18:1-12, we find an immediate answer to Jesus' prayer in John 17. Jesus went to a private place in the garden to pray. Prayer was such a priority to Jesus that he took His disciples to a regular spot in the Garden of Gethsemane. Judas knew this place of prayer because he had prayed in the garden. This place of powerful prayer became a place of betrayal. In the Old Testament, a place of prayer became a place of betrayal for Daniel, and a place of power. It was a place of betrayal because his enemies knew that he was faithful to pray each day in that spot. It was a place of power because his faithful prayers had victorious results. Like Daniel, Jesus prayed faithfully in the garden.

Judas betrayed Jesus. In John 18:3, the Bible says that he led "a detachment of soldiers and some officials from the chief priests and the Pharisees...carrying torches, lanterns, and weapons."

I cannot give you the exact number of who were in the garden at this exact moment. Scholars give a wide range for the number of soldiers in the kind of "detachment" mentioned in this verse. A cohort of Roman soldiers was typically six hundred men, but the number could vary widely and sometimes include as few as two hundred men.[9] However, commentators are specific that there were Roman soldiers there in the garden: "The band, or cohort, was from the Roman garrison in the tower of Antonia."[10]

I do not know the exact number of actors present in the garden on that night, but I can tell you that this moment was like a gas-filled room, ready to burst into flames. With just a single spark, the whole

[9] Barclay Moon Newman and Eugene Albert Nida, A Handbook on the Gospel of John, United Bible Societies Handbooks (New York: United Bible Societies, 1993).

[10] Marvin Richardson Vincent, Word Studies in the New Testament, vol. 2 (New York: Charles Scribner's Sons, 1887).

situation would have exploded. Everyone who was present—Jesus, His disciples, the Roman guards, the religious leaders, Judas, the disciple Peter—had a different agenda. All these people were gathered in a very small part of the garden. I think this space was like a tinderbox or a powder keg: ready to explode.

In Matthew 26:47-50, we read, "Judas, one of the Twelve, arrived. With him was a large crowd armed with swords and clubs, sent from the chief priests and the elders of the people. Now the betrayer had arranged a signal with them: 'The one I kiss is the man; arrest him.' Going at once to Jesus, Judas said, 'Greetings, Rabbi!' and kissed him. Jesus replied, 'Friend, do what you came for.'" Judas betrayed Jesus with a kiss, an intimate relational sign. Judas acted as if he had Yada (an intimate relationship) with Jesus, but we see as we study his life that he acted within the constraints of Gnosis.

John 18:4: …knowing all that would happen to him…. Jesus knew what Judas was there to do in the garden. What was Jesus's personal agenda that night? I believe that He was there to ensure a peaceful resolution in that moment and future moments. He wanted to emphatically declare, "If the world is against you, the Trinity is for you. The world will bow to the will of the Father."

In the garden, many were against Jesus. He was managing a powder keg ready to blow. Peter, with his hot-tempered personality, was not being helpful. In John 18:10, we read that "Simon Peter, who had a sword, drew it and struck the high priest's servant, cutting off his right ear." Why did Jesus then rebuke Peter and then heal the servant's ear? I believe that He knew that one spark would set off the majority who were there to kill Him and His followers. Remember the last theology that I taught you? Jesus did not want to lose even one disciple.

In John 17, Jesus prayed for His disciples present and future. In John 18, we see the answer to those prayers. The enemy was furious and had provoked a group to kill Jesus. The spark that set off the group could have been Peter and his swordplay. Can you see the power exhibited by the Trinity in this moment? The spark occurred when Peter lopped off Malchus's ear. Jesus rebuked Peter while perfectly restoring the ear. Can you even imagine seeing someone's ear replaced in the middle of everything else that was occurring? The omnipotent God peacefully directed the moment.

As a part of the Trinity, Jesus has the characteristics of omniscience and omnipotence. This is a tension in the Bible that we must maintain even if we do not comprehend it. I must admit, this idea warrants further investigation. Jesus could not win this battle by being one hundred percent divine. He had to win the battle being one hundred percent human—a human trusting in the Trinity.

I have already given you an example of humanity trusting the Trinity in the chapter on the theology of God's provision. Jesus taught His human disciples to depend on the Trinity to accomplish the miraculous. There are humans who lay hands on the sick and the sick recover. We see this marvel often in the Bible and around our world. Miracles like these are accomplished by humans trusting the Trinity. The baptism of Jesus was performed with human hands, but the Trinity was present. I give these examples to say that Jesus was one hundred percent human in the garden as He depended on the Trinity.

The Gospel of John shows Jesus in control. Everyone against Jesus was powerless to accomplish their desired agendas. Now slow down. I want you to understand this thought. Jesus came to give His life to us; nobody was going to take His life. If those who were against Jesus took his life, the eternal outcome would have been permanently destroyed. This moment in time was pivotal and deserves more research, time, and discussion.

These scriptures in John 18 demonstrate the foolishness of humankind—those who are in the process of believing, like Peter, and those who do not believe in Jesus. Think about what is transpiring in the garden during this prickly, dangerous, and explosive moment. Jesus asked someone, one of the many there to kill Him, "Who is it you want?" The reply was, "Jesus of Nazareth." You must be kidding me! This man was full of hatred and a desire to kill. As he was looking into Jesus's eyes, his answer to the question "who do you want?" was "Jesus." Imagine asking someone, "who do you want?" and that person looking into your eyes and saying your name. You would know that the person had no clue who you were. Think about the senselessness of that moment.

John 18:4-6: Jesus, knowing all that was going to happen to him, went out and asked them, "Who is it you want?" "Jesus of Nazareth," they replied. "I am he," Jesus said. (And Judas the traitor was standing there with them.) When Jesus said, "I am he," they drew back and fell to the ground. Think about the power of Jesus's words and their Trinity connection. When the men in the garden responded that they wanted Jesus, Jesus replied, "I Am He!" When they heard that response from Jesus, "they" fell to the ground like dead men." I am not sure who "they" refers to. Was it the religious leaders, their guards, Judas, or just the Roman soldiers? If "they" meant the Roman soldiers—powerful, powerful, strong men with authority and weapons—everyone must have suddenly stopped breathing. The only spoken word that rang out in the thick and explosive silence was "I am he."

I will mention here that the account in John 18 represents the second battle in a garden in the Bible. We encounter the first garden battle in Genesis, in the Garden of Eden. Here, humans miserably lost the battle for their souls to the enemy. Defeat! In John 18, the second garden battle, Jesus won a decisive blow for the souls of all humanity! Victory! I believe that this battle had to be won by Jesus using His one hundred percent humanity.

There are many "I Am" statements written in the Old and New Testaments. The Old Testament contains the "I Am" statements of God, while the New Testament reveals the "I Am" statements of Jesus. The "I Am" of Jesus in John 18 is my favorite. I love the connection that is found between God and Jesus. This (and many other connections) speaks to the unity between the Old and New Testaments and the Trinity.

I cannot believe that the absurdity of this moment continued, but Jesus asked them again, "Who do you want?" The response was the same, "Jesus." Jesus responded once again, "I am he." This time they did not fall to the ground. I believe when the omnipotent God spoke—I will give my life and you will not take my life—they were convinced of His power and abandoned their plan to kill Him. The Father and Son agreed on the final plan. Jesus says in John 10:17-18, "'The reason my Father loves me is that I lay down my life—only to take it up again. No one takes it from me, but I lay it down of my own accord.'"

Those that wanted to dispose of Jesus knew that it was not possible. Jesus would give His own life; nobody would take it from him. The Roman soldiers knew nothing of the Word of God, but the religious leaders sure did. Why didn't they speak up against Christ?

I warn you that some commentators do not believe that what I am about to share with you is connected. This connection may need more research, but I see a connection and want to present it to you.

When Jesus said, "I am He," I believed that the Trinity reconnected. When Jesus stated, "I am He," He connected to His Father who said the same phrase. In Exodus 3:14, God says to Moses, "'I AM WHO I AM. This is what you are to say to the Israelites: "I AM has sent me to you."'" I believe that Jesus used this phrase to make the connection with the Trinity (specifically the Father) and the power of the Trinity. When Jesus declared to the crowd in John 18:5, "I am he," and the Father declared to Moses in Exodus 3:14, "I AM," the Father and Son became one in the human realm as they are one in the heavenly realm.

This thought becomes clearer when read Jesus's words in John 10:30: "I and the Father are one." Even before this, the Trinity had already spoken the truth of this relationship in John 1:18. John wrote of Jesus, "No one has ever seen God, but the one and only Son, who is himself God and is in closest relationship with the Father, has made him known." Jesus spoke many times about His unity with the Father. When He spoke this truth, He was always attacked for speaking blasphemy. Curiously, that attack did not occur when Jesus declared, "I am," in the second garden battle.

Not one of the religious leaders present in the garden refuted Jesus's statement. That was their moment. They had been wanting to prove Jesus a heretic! Jesus once more connected Himself with the Father. They could have shouted, "heretic!" from the rooftops, but they were strangely silent there in the garden. Could it be that it was impossible for the religious leaders to argue after a demonstration of Godly power through Jesus, a demonstration that invoked His true identity, "I Am He"?

Jesus also said "I Am He" in John 8:28: "'When you have lifted up the Son of Man, then you will know that I am he.'" Everyone who witnessed Calvary understood the true identity and power of the triune God.

In both the Old and New Testaments there were demonstrations of the omnipotent Trinity. No one doubted who was speaking! When Jesus made his two "I am" statements in John 18, if anyone could doubt Jesus was making a powerful connection with His Father, it would be the religious leaders. They were ready to rebuke Him, kill Him, and destroy any memory of Christ in Israel. I believe they must have fallen to the ground too. I like to think that those who were against Jesus were a part of group that was pushed to the ground.

I will show you in the Old Testament that the Father used the same "I Am" phrase before He rescued the Jewish slaves. In Exodus 6:6, God says, "'Therefore, say to the Israelites: "I am the Lord, and I will bring you out from under the yoke of the Egyptians. I will free you from being slaves to them, and I will redeem you with an outstretched arm and with mighty acts of judgment."'" The Father told Moses that the powerful Yahweh would free His chosen people from slavery in Egypt with many proofs of His power. Questions such as "who are You, God?" and "what is the meaning of this thing You did?" are Yada questions. Exodus 13:14 says, "'In days to come, when your son asks you, "What does this mean?" say to him, "With a mighty hand the Lord brought us out of Egypt, out of the land of slavery."'"

Many times, Yada questions in the Bible come from children being trained about God by their parents. In John 18, Jesus showed His disciples with one powerful proof that He would free all of humanity from the slavery of sin. Jesus extended His Father's love from a specific group of people (the Israelites) to all of humanity.

Jesus created the habit of prayer in the garden with His disciples. Then He invited His core disciples to witness His powerful connection to the Father. Finally, He demonstrated proof that He was giving His life to free the world from sin. The disciples had no doubt that Jesus purposefully connected Himself with the Father. Many lose sight of Jesus in the Old Testament. Some wonder if the Trinity formula is present if Jesus is not mentioned. But when you consider John 1:1, you see that the Trinity connection has been evident since before the beginning of time.

Chapter Eleven:
T3D International Workbook

Use a separate piece of paper and try to answer the three questions. Then please fill in the blanks. This will be the last workbook that you will need to complete for my course. You must continue reading the book until the last chapter.

1. What theology can you observe in John 18:1-12?

2. What did you learn about God in this chapter?

3. What did you learn about what God wants from you in this chapter?

I am going to explore some of the verses in John 18 and expound on some theologies that I observe in verses 1-12.

John 18:1-12

"When he had finished praying, Jesus left with his disciples and crossed the Kidron Valley. On the other side there was a garden, and he and his disciples went into it. Now Judas, who betrayed him, knew the place, because Jesus had often met there with his disciples. So Judas came to the garden, guiding a detachment of soldiers and some officials from the chief priests and the Pharisees. They were carrying torches, lanterns, and weapons. Jesus, knowing all that was going to happen to him, went out and asked them, 'Who is it you want?' 'Jesus of Nazareth,' they replied. 'I am he,' Jesus said. (And Judas the traitor was standing there with them.) When Jesus said, 'I am he,' they drew back and fell to the ground. Again, he asked them, 'Who is it you want?' 'Jesus of Nazareth,' they said. Jesus answered, 'I told you that I am he. If you are looking for me, then let these men go.' This happened so that the words he had spoken would be fulfilled: 'I have not lost one of those you gave me.' Then

Simon Peter, who had a sword, drew it, and struck the high priest's servant, cutting off his right ear. (The servant's name was Malchus.) Jesus commanded Peter, 'Put your sword away! Shall I not drink the cup the Father has given me?' Then the detachment of soldiers with its commander and the Jewish officials arrested Jesus."

John 18:1: "When he had finished praying." When you read that, your question should have been, "what did He _____ about?" Read the Bible with a thirst to know what the Lord has to say. Take a quick peek at John 17:9, 11-12, 15, and 20 to understand what He prayed about. You are the _____ Jesus mentions in this prayer. The Trinity loves you.

In John 18:1-12, we find an immediate answer to Jesus' prayer in John 17. Jesus went to a private place in the _____ to pray. Prayer was such a priority to Jesus that he took His disciples to a _____ in the Garden of Gethsemane. Judas knew this place of prayer because he had prayed in the garden. This place of powerful prayer became a place of _____. In the Old Testament, a place of prayer became a place of betrayal for Daniel, and a place of power. It was a place of betrayal because his _____ knew that he was _____ to pray each day in that spot. It was a place of power because his faithful prayers had _____. Like Daniel, Jesus prayed faithfully in the garden.

Judas betrayed Jesus. In John 18:3, the Bible says that he led "a _____ of soldiers and some officials from the chief priests and the Pharisees...carrying torches, lanterns, and weapons."

I cannot give you the exact number of who were in the garden at this exact moment. Scholars give a wide range for the number of soldiers in the kind of "detachment" mentioned in this verse. A cohort of Roman soldiers was typically six hundred men, but the number could vary widely and sometimes include as few as two hundred men.[11] However, commentators are specific that there were Roman _____ there in the garden: "The band, or cohort, was from the Roman garrison in the tower of Antonia."[12]

I do not know the exact number of actors present in the garden on that night, but I can tell you that this moment was like a gas-filled room, ready to burst into flames. With just a single spark, the whole situation would have _____. Everyone who was present— Jesus, His disciples, the Roman guards, the religious leaders, Judas, the disciple Peter—had a different agenda. All these people were gathered in a very small part of the garden. I think this space was like a tinderbox or a powder keg: ready to explode.

In Matthew 26:47-50, we read, "Judas, one of the Twelve, arrived. With him was a large crowd armed with swords and clubs, sent from the chief priests and the elders of the people. Now the betrayer had arranged a signal with them: 'The one I _____ is the man; arrest him.' Going at once to Jesus, Judas said, 'Greetings, Rabbi!' and kissed him. Jesus replied, 'Friend, do what you came for.'" Judas betrayed

[11] Barclay Moon Newman and Eugene Albert Nida, A Handbook on the Gospel of John, United Bible Societies Handbooks (New York: United Bible Societies, 1993).

[12] Marvin Richardson Vincent, Word Studies in the New Testament, vol. 2 (New York: Charles Scribner's Sons, 1887).

Jesus with a kiss, an intimate relational sign. Judas acted as if he had Yada (an intimate relationship) with Jesus, but we see as we study his life that he acted within the constraints of Gnosis.

John 18:4: ...knowing all that would happen to him.... Jesus knew what Judas was there to do in the garden. What was Jesus's personal agenda that night? I believe that He was there to ensure a _____ in that moment and future moments. He wanted to emphatically declare, "If the world is against you, the Trinity is for you. The world will bow to the will of the Father."

In the garden, many were against Jesus. He was managing a powder keg ready to blow. Peter, with his hot-tempered personality, was not being helpful. In John 18:10, we read that "Simon Peter, who had a sword, drew it and _____ the high priest's servant, cutting off his right ear." Why did Jesus then rebuke Peter and then heal the servant's ear? I believe that He knew that one spark would set off the majority who were there to kill Him and His followers. Remember the last theology that I taught you? Jesus did not want to lose even one disciple.

In John 17, Jesus prayed for His disciples present and future. In John 18, we see the answer to those prayers. The enemy was furious and had _____ a group to kill Jesus. The spark that set off the group could have been Peter and his swordplay. Can you see the power exhibited by the Trinity in this moment? The spark occurred when Peter lopped off Malchus's ear. Jesus rebuked Peter while perfectly

_____ the ear. Can you even imagine seeing someone's ear replaced in the middle of everything else that was occurring? The God peacefully directed the moment.

The Gospel of John shows Jesus in control. Everyone against Jesus was powerless to accomplish their _____. Now slow down. I want you to understand this thought. Jesus came to _____ His life to us; nobody was going to _____ His life. If those who were against Jesus took his life, the eternal _____ would have been permanently _____. This moment in time was pivotal to God's creation and deserves more research, time, and discussion.

Jesus asked someone, one of the many there to kill Him, "_____ is it you want?" The reply was, "_____ of Nazareth." You must be kidding me! This man was full of hatred and a desire to kill. As he was looking into Jesus's eyes, his answer to the question "who do you want?" was "Jesus." Imagine asking someone, "who do you want?" and that person looking into your eyes and saying your name. You would know that the person had no clue who you were. Think about the senselessness of that moment.

John 18:4-6: Jesus, knowing all that was going to happen to him, went out and asked them, "Who is it you want?" "Jesus of Nazareth," they replied. "I am he," Jesus said. (And Judas the traitor was standing there with them.) When Jesus said, "I am he," they drew back and fell to the ground. Think about the power of Jesus's words and their Trinity connection. When the men in the garden responded that they wanted Jesus, Jesus replied,

"_____!" When they heard that response from Jesus, "they" fell to the ground like _____." I am not sure who "they" refers to. Was it the religious leaders, their guards, Judas, or just the Roman soldiers? If "they" meant the Roman soldiers—powerful, powerful, strong men with authority and weapons—everyone must have suddenly _____ breathing. The only spoken word that rang out in the dark and explosive silence was "I am he."

I will mention here that the account in John 18 represents the second battle in a garden in the Bible. We encounter the first garden _____ in Genesis, in the Garden of Eden. Here, humans miserably _____ the battle for their souls to the enemy. Defeat! In John 18, the _____ garden battle, Jesus _____ a decisive blow for the souls of all humanity! Victory! I believe that this battle had to be won by Jesus using His one hundred percent humanity.

There are many "I Am" statements written in the Old and New Testaments. The Old Testament contains the "I Am" statements of _____, while the New Testament reveals the "I Am" statements of _____. The "I Am" of Jesus in John 18 is my favorite. I love the connection that is found between God and Jesus. This (and many other connections) speaks to the unity between the Old and New Testaments and the Trinity.

I cannot believe that the absurdity of this moment continued, but Jesus asked them again, "Who do you want?" The _____ was the same, "Jesus." Jesus responded once again, "I am he." This time they did not fall to the ground. I believe when the omnipotent God spoke—I will give my life and you will not take my life—they were of His power and _____ their plan to kill Him. The Father and Son agreed on the final plan. Jesus says in John 10:17-18, "'The reason my Father loves me is that I _____down my life—only to _____ up again. No one takes it from me, but I lay it down of my own accord.'"

Those that wanted to dispose of Jesus knew that it was _____. Jesus would give His own life; nobody would take it from him. The Roman soldiers knew nothing of the Word of God, but the ____ leaders sure did. Why didn't they speak up against Christ?

I warn you that some commentators do not believe that what I am about to share with you is connected. This connection may need more research, but I see a _____ and want to present it to you.

When Jesus said, "I Am He," I believed that the Trinity _____. When Jesus stated, "I am He," He connected to His Father who said the same phrase. In Exodus 3:14, God says to _____, "'I AM WHO I AM. This is what you are to say to the Israelites: "I AM has sent me to you."'" I believe that Jesus _____ this phrase to make the connection with the Trinity (specifically the Father) and the power of the Trinity. When Jesus declared to the crowd in John 18:5, "I am he," and the Father declared to Moses in Exodus 3:14, "I AM," the Father and Son _____ in the human realm as they are one in the heavenly realm.

Not one of the religious leaders present in the garden _____ Jesus's statement. That was their moment. They had been wanting to Jesus a heretic! Jesus once more connected Himself with the Father. They could have shouted, "_____!" from the rooftops, but they were strangely _____ there in the garden. Could it be that it was impossible for the religious leaders to argue after a _____ of Godly power through Jesus, a demonstration that invoked His true identity, "I Am He"?

In John 18, Jesus showed His disciples with one powerful proof that He would free all of humanity from the slavery of sin. Jesus extended His Father's love from a specific group of people (the Israelites) to all of _____. The enemy lost his death grip over humanity.

Jesus created the _____ of prayer in the garden with His disciples. Then He invited His core disciples to _____ His powerful connection to the Father. Finally, He demonstrated _____ that He was giving His life to _____ the world from _____. The disciples had no doubt that Jesus purposefully connected Himself with the Father. Many lose sight of Jesus in the Old Testament. Some wonder if the Trinity formula is present if Jesus is not mentioned. But when you consider John 1:1, you see that the Trinity connection has been _____ since before the beginning of time.

Thank you for taking the time to fill in the blanks! I hope the theologies have simmered in your heart as you reviewed the material twice. You will become an expert teacher when you teach this book to others. Continue on to Chapter Twelve, an essential chapter for all T3D disciples! This chapter will solidify what you have learned by allowing you to apply it in a practical way.

Chapter Twelve:
The Social/Evangelistic Project

Why do you need to complete a T3D International Social/Evangelistic Project? This is part of the Yada experience. Plan to do a project for God and for the benefit of others. Plan to provoke a Yada response. The recipients of your project should ask you, "Who is your God?" They will ask you, "Why would you do this project for me?"

Think about doing your first Social/Evangelistic Project locally. This will save time and finances for you. If you are planning your T3D International Social/Evangelistic Project alone, it does not need to cost a lot of money (or any money). If you are planning your T3D International Social/Evangelistic Project as a group, your project does not need to cost a lot (or cost any money) individually. Divide up the costs within your team.

Plan a simple Social/Evangelistic Project that you can complete in one hour. For now, do not create an ongoing ministry. All you need to do is to complete a project. It is possible that after you graduate from T3D International, you can create an ongoing ministry with the Lord if you like the project you created.

T3D International discipleship teams work together for three months. They study, work, evangelize, do their project, and finally graduate together. In the middle of these three months, individuals or teams must use their own ideas and finances to develop a Social/Evangelistic Project within their city. Accomplishing a Social/Evangelistic Project by yourself can be a daunting task if you have never planned one before. If you are working by yourself, use my book to learn about how to plan for this project. If you are learning about this material by studying as a team, it may be easier to achieve. Use everyone's talents to accomplish the project. The Holy Spirit has given you these talents so that you will use them for Him!

Since the Social/Evangelistic Project involves the word "evangelistic," I want to give you a thought on that topic. Your project is going to stir the hearts of people you do not know yet. Do not use this opportunity to force someone into a relationship with God. You can, however, creatively share a verse from Chapter Six.

This project will be a moment where God wants to touch hearts. That is why you must do a creative project that provoke the question, "Who is your God?" If you sense that someone is touched by the Lord, continue to pray for that person by name, and go back and carefully grow that relationship. Do not abandon that person. Continue to work with them over time.

I want to assure you that groups can create their own projects if they want. I will include examples of past projects to help you with brainstorming. Again, you are not obligated to choose from these examples, but you can repeat them if you would like.

Example Project 1:
Uruguay Roof

I was asked to preach at Uber's church in Salto, Uruguay. After I preached the service, a young man popped up and walked straight toward me. As he approached, he asked me if I knew him. Since I am a New Yorker, I jokingly asked him, "Why? Do I owe you money?" He said no. He asked me if I was the one that trained groups to go and help people in the community. I told him yes, all my groups were learning how to do Social/Evangelistic Projects to help their community. The young man shared with me that last weekend, one of the T3D teams found out that every time it rained, his roof leaked on his baby's bed. He and his wife were overwhelmed when the group of five disciples used their own money and spent the next four hours putting a new roof on his small house. The man had attended the service that morning to find the answer to his question: "Who is your God?" Below, you will see photos of the roof work in Uruguay. Joy appeared through the disciples' smiles as they worked. This is the joy that I am trying to create in all the ministries that you do for the Lord!

It is said that a religious pastor keeps you busy within the four walls of the church, while a kingdom pastor trains, equips, and deploys you outside the church to transform your community and nation.

The team that fixed the young man's roof certainly went outside the church to transform their community! You will also embody this quote as you touch others where they live for the Trinity. Going to do the Social/ Evangelistic Project moves you purposefully outside the walls of your church and toward the people in need of a God who is here for them.

Left: T3D disciples repair a family's roof."

Bottom: T3D disciples take a picture with the family."

Example Project 2:
Ecuador Children's Hospital

In 2022, I taught T3D International for three months in Quito, Ecuador, training one hundred leaders. One of my twenty groups of five disciples had a difficult time deciding what to do for their Social/Evangelistic Project. I told the class that they did not need to use money for the project, they just needed to do something unexpected so that the recipient would ask the Yada question, "Who is your God?" I mentioned that they could go to the children's hospital (Baca Ortiz) and minister to the parents who came to visit their dying children, as long as what they did was heartfelt and representative of God's Yada love.

The group liked this idea, but they did not know what to do, so they prayed to God for direction. Remember that Covid restrictions were still enforced in Ecuador in 2022. As the team trusted God, He allowed them to encounter a single mom who was taking care of her daughter, Amelia, who had been admitted to Baca Ortiz with leukemia, a blood cancer with no known cure. The mother was the only family member giving care to her little girl.

The team started to minister to Amelia's mom by writing individual letters to her, telling her how valiant she was and that she was appreciated by people she did not even know. Some members of the team gave special gifts and open letters to the mom for her to give to Amelia. These teams in Ecuador are very poor, but some of the team members gave their food money to the mom. The team promised to pray for the mom and Amelia. The mom sat with Amelia and told her that a group of people were praying for her and that they had given them some money. She and her daughter wondered, "Why would someone want to do this for us?" In truth, the question is, "Who is your God and what does He mean by your actions? Why does He love us?" For a moment, because of a T3D International Social/Evangelistic Project, God showed His intimate love for a mom and her daughter.

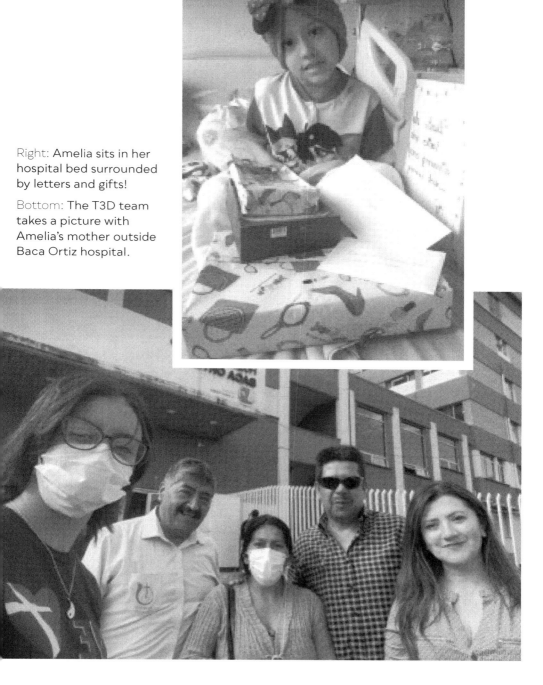

Right: Amelia sits in her hospital bed surrounded by letters and gifts!

Bottom: The T3D team takes a picture with Amelia's mother outside Baca Ortiz hospital.

Example Project 3:
Recycling Cart

Cris's team in Sangolqui, Ecuador, saw a poor family—mother, father, and children—entering neighborhood dumpsters. The small children were lowered into the dumpster so they could throw all the materials that could be recycled to their parents. The parents would haul huge bags from dumpster to dumpster. Near the end of the day, the bag was so heavy that it took the entire family to drag it. Cris came up with the creative idea to weld a cart from scratch. The T3D International team, along with Cris's wife Erika and Cris's father, bought tires and materials and welded a cart with walls that could contain all the recycling for the day. The wheels made the cart easy to manage. When the team finished painting the cart, they filled it with recycled materials and brought it to the family. The family had no words! Their eyes and hearts asked the question, "Why us? Who is your God?" The cart has been seen around the neighborhood with smiling faces pushing it.

The family with their new cart!

Example Project 4:
New Window

A team in Uruguay told me that they knew about a poor family and wanted to buy food for them. I told them that this kindness might not provoke a Yada response. My response made them curious, so they asked, "What should we do for the family?" I told them to ask the family directly what they needed. Upon asking the family, the team was told that their desire to give food was appreciated, but that it was not what the family needed. The T3D team was surprised. The family had a small house with many children. They had built the house over time but had never had enough money to put a window in the concrete wall. So, what do you think the team did? They installed a window. When the team finished the work, the family asked, "Who is your God? Why did you do this for us?"

Example Project 5:
Lunch and Gifts

I am personally doing two Social/Evangelistic projects each year here in Ecuador. One project I do at the end of each year and involve disciples that I have trained. They help me give lunch and a traditional Christmas gift to four thousand children, between the ages of three and fourteen. The people who live on the coast here are the poorest of the poor in Ecuador. This event is the first time that many of the children have ever received a gift. The parents usually ask, "Who is your God? Why would you do this?"

Example Project 6:
Supplies Scholarships

In honor of my wife Denise, I have created a scholarship for children ages fifteen to seventeen. These children are required to pay for their own school supplies. The children work outside of the house and their parents try to pay these costs. In two coastal cities, I have my trained T3D International leaders ask students from various high schools to submit a scholarship request. It is important that they show their grades and have a good GPA. The children that gain the scholarship are invited to a lunch and receive a certificate signed by their parents. I wanted the parents to understand that their child is working hard and doing well in school. At the lunch, each child is given a scholarship of thirty dollars to buy school supplies. The teenagers and their parents have a Yada response: "Who is your God, and why would you do this?" In 2023, I was able to give one hundred scholarships.

All these projects are examples of making disciples "in your going." As you live life, be kind. It is possible that as you follow up with the people you ministered during your project, someone may want to interact with the command of the Trinity and become a disciple.

Whatever project you do, be creative! Do something that will elicit the Yada question: "Who is your God, why does He love me, and why are you doing this for me?" The Social/Evangelistic Project is not about giving a dollar to a poor person on the street. That gesture is kind, but most times it does not elicit the Yada response. A book called *Conspiracy of Kindness* by Steve Sjogren has many creative ideas that can be used for your Social/Evangelistic Project if you have trouble choosing one.[13] I prefer that you and your team think and pray about a project that makes sense in your local culture.

During this project, you and your team must also share the gospel in a simple way. Use the scriptures that I gave you in Chapter Six. You can make your own tracts with one of those scriptures to make your project culturally relevant. Remember that you are doing a Social/EVANGELISTIC Project. Everyone who believes in the scriptures you present will be saved. You are not ashamed of the gospel, are you? (Romans 1:16). In my mind, discipleship and evangelism go hand in hand. You will find this idea to be true when you complete your Social/Evangelistic Project with the goal of demonstrating the love of God to those who are lost.

---

[13] Steve Sjogren, Conspiracy of Kindness: A Unique Approach to Sharing the Love of Jesus, Revised and Updated (Ada, Michigan: Baker Publishing Group, 2008).

Evangelism should always be accomplished with a correct and loving heart. A correct heart is what we learned in Luke 8: a joyful heart. Instead of running after people to evangelize them, it is easier to have them running after you asking, "Who is your God?" A question like that comes after you have tangibility loved someone by giving to them with no agenda. This is how you love people into God's kingdom.

I love Luke 10:17: "the seventy-two returned with joy." This verse is central to your T3D International Social/Evangelistic Project. How strange that seventy-two disciples went out to help others using their own strength, time, and funds, yet they returned with joy! The Lord will give you joy as you sacrificially work for the benefit of others. God blesses both the receiver and the giver of sacrificial love with the joy of knowing Him. He loves you as His disciple, as he loves all who have great needs.

I have found that as I train T3D International disciples, the Holy Spirit influences them to become others-oriented. When I did my doctoral research, I discovered that sixty church members who participated in my study viewed the Holy Spirit from a self-oriented perspective. They viewed the Holy Spirit as a kind of personal assistant, someone to care for and teach them. The book of Acts informs us that once we are filled with the Spirit, God pushes us outside the walls of our churches.

I want to help you as a disciple to discover a correct understanding of the role of the Holy Spirit. Yes, He is there to aid us personally. He is the paraclete, as Jesus mentions in John 14:26: "But the Advocate, the Holy Spirit, whom the Father will send in my name, will teach you all things and will remind you of everything I have said to you." We understand this idea. What we are missing is that the Spirit will move us out of our comfort zones for the good of others. This book has mostly concentrated on the Holy Spirit's purposes outside of ourselves.

Since there is no salvation without the heartfelt conviction of the Holy Spirit, the fruit of the Spirit must be present if we are to evangelize effectively. Galatians 5:22-23 lists the fruit of the Spirit: "love, joy, peace, patience, kindness, goodness, faithfulness, gentleness, and self-control."

Research the thief on the cross who went to paradise according to Jesus's word. While the thief endured the cruel event of being hung on a cross, Jesus demonstrated the most basic evangelism I can find in the Bible. Can you determine if the fruit of the Spirit was present? Our loving God shows His love even to criminals, even to the last moments of a misused life. Even as this thief hung on the cross, the presence of the Holy Spirit was evident. Try to name the fruits of the Holy Spirit. He is present in the process of salvation. Jesus told the man, "Today you will be with me in paradise" (Luke 23:43).

Every disciple on your team must participate in the Social/Evangelistic Project in one way or another. The Holy Spirit pours out His anointing in a special way as you "go" and do His will sacrificially for others. You will produce creative ideas as you brainstorm for this project. Do not be concerned if you repeat one of the projects that has already been done. This is just a start for you and your disciples. It is important to start. Once you get the idea, keep making disciples and keep creating Social/Evangelistic Projects. You just need to complete one project before you can graduate from the T3D International course.

Evangelism must be accomplished sacrificially in a community of disciples through Social/Evangelistic Projects, with the love of the Father and the empowerment of the Holy Spirit. Organizing a church into teams of evangelizing disciples is a powerful strategy because of the dynamics of the strength of the team. The team's unity dispels individual fears of failure and rejection, which are common feelings when people are ministering to unreached people. Team unity also creates a safe environment for the individual members to explore and utilize their talents and spiritual gifts. Furthermore, something powerful happens when the disciples support the project with their own ideas and finances—they feel empowered and valued as disciples, and the people they are reaching also gain a sense of being valued.

After a Social/Evangelistic Project, it is much easier to evangelize to people who do not currently recognize the peace of Jesus in their hearts. After they have seen an act of love personally demonstrated to them, it is easier for them to ask Jesus to forgive their sins and live in their hearts. Many times, people will ask the question "Who is your God?" It is much easier to bring lost souls to Jesus if they ask you this question directly. Instead of chasing them with the gospel, you just need to answer their question. If you do your Social/Evangelistic Project correctly, you will be answering that question often.

Chapter Thirteen:
Evangelism and Discipleship

T3D International pairs Evangelism and Discipleship together. Classical Trinitarian theology is evangelistic and relational. You need to constantly evangelize new believers before you can disciple them. However, there has been a lack of care for the new believer. Often, new believers have no one to disciple them. This is like unharvested fruit falling off the branch and deteriorating on the ground. T3D International teaches disciples how to use the Romans Road scriptures to evangelize others. Jesus Himself used a model that combined discipleship and evangelism. In Mark 1:16-20, He told His first disciples that He would make them fishers of men, both disciples and evangelists.

A new movement is alive. As you read this book, you are a part of a Classical Trinitarian movement, an evangelical movement inspired by the Bible that believes the Bible guides the conduct of believers. The entire Bible is to be interpreted as instructions for the believer's life. I believe that the teaching of the book of Acts is to be lived out by each Christian disciple. Faith in the Bible empowers T3D International.

Two fundamental truths are integral in the T3D International strategy: the Trinity and Spirit baptism. Both the Trinity and Spirit baptism are evident in the life of Jesus during His baptism. This event is recorded in Matthew 3:16: "As soon as Jesus was baptized, he went up out of the water. At that moment heaven was opened, and he saw the Spirit of God descending like a dove and alighting on him." Jesus's baptism is confirmed in Acts 10:37-38: "'You know what has happened throughout the province of Judea, beginning in Galilee after the baptism that John preached—how God anointed Jesus of Nazareth with the Holy Spirit and power, and how he went around doing good and healing all who were under the power of the devil, because God was with him.'" These two scriptures are central to T3D International and a Classical Trinitarian theological approach to forming future disciples. Jesus was baptized in water by John the Baptist. The scripture announces that the Spirit (like a dove) alighted on Jesus. The Father, Son, and Holy Spirit were all present at His baptism.

As disciples, we have the blessing of inviting the Holy Spirit to empower us. One of the strengths of T3D International is a strategy to ask for the infilling of the Holy Spirit to be given to disciples so they can train others as Jesus commanded in Matthew 28:19.

Look how similar Acts 10:37-38 are to Acts 1:8. Acts 10:37-38 says, "'You know what has happened throughout the province of Judea, beginning in Galilee after the baptism that John preached—how God anointed Jesus of Nazareth with the Holy Spirit and power, and how he went around doing good and healing all who were under the power of the devil, because God was with him.'" These verses confirm the life of Jesus after the Holy Spirit alighted on and empowered Him. Jesus ministered in Galilee and Judea and to regions further away, just as Jesus tells His disciples in Acts 1:8 to preach in Judea, Samaria, and the ends of the earth.

I recommend that you read all of Acts 10; you will discover that the Trinity formula is mentioned four times. For now, I want to expound on Acts 10:37-38.

Luke wrote the Gospel of Luke and the book of Acts. In Acts 10:37, Peter is speaking, and he makes a general statement: you all know what has happened in our area of the world. The Trinity made quite a spiritual stir at Jesus' baptism. Everyone around knew what happened.

I also want to draw your attention to a few details you may have missed in Acts 10:38: "*God* anointed *Jesus* of Nazareth with the *Holy Spirit* and power" (emphasis mine). This verse contains one of the four Trinity formulas in Acts 10. You should be aware that the Father anointed Jesus with the Holy Spirit and power. Did the Trinity do this amongst themselves? I believe that Jesus walked the earth as one hundred percent human, but we also know that He is one hundred percent Trinity. Jesus, like us, needed to depend on the Holy Spirit.

We can do what Jesus did and more as we depend on the Trinity. Jesus tells his disciples in John 14:12-14, "Very truly I tell you, whoever believes in me will do the works I have been doing, and they will do even greater things than these, because I am going to the Father.

And I will do whatever you ask in my name, so that the Father may be glorified in the Son. You may ask me for anything in my name, and I will do it." We need to meditate a long time about what it really means to be anointed with the Holy Spirit and power.

Let's consider another section of Acts 10:38: "he went around doing good and healing all." this part of the verse describes what happened after the Father anointed Jesus with the Holy Spirit and power. Jesus's first thoughts may not have been "now I have someone to guide Me." It appears that His first thought was to use the power of the Holy Spirit to meet the needs of others.

These are scriptures that motivated my writing of T3D International. I am trying to make disciples who make disciples, who make disciples. Our first thoughts should be to train others to reach into a dark world with the power of His Spirit. As a disciple, you must endeavor to reflect the Trinity and accomplish His desires toward people in need. Do good and heal in His name.

Acts 10:38 ends with the phrase "God was with him." Again, this is a Biblical tension we must ponder. Luke is not saying that the Trinity was with Jesus. I am saying that God was with Jesus as He walked on the earth as He was one hundred percent human. This makes sense to me because as a human, I need God to be with me. I am not sure that we truly understand this thought. If we are to make T3D International disciples and go into a dark world to touch people for Him, we need the Trinity and the fullness of His power.

Now let's examine Acts 1:8: "But you will receive power when the Holy Spirit comes on you; and you will be my witnesses in Jerusalem, and in all Judea and Samaria, and to the ends of the earth." In Acts 1:8, we are given permission by Jesus to ask for a divine touch. Ask God to fill us as He filled His Son with the Holy Spirit and power. This verse describes Spiritual baptism only. This Spiritual baptism should yield the results that Jesus experienced. Our first thoughts should be about serving others. Look what Jesus told us in Acts 1:8: "you will be my witnesses."

The original Greek word for "witnesses" is the word "martyrs." In Acts 1:8, you are invited to be God's martyrs. Giving your life away is a one-time gift. There is no better way to tell people that you love them with the love of the Trinity than to give your life away as a martyr. Jesus did exactly that—shouldn't we do the same as His disciples?

I believe that the word "martyr" has a dual meaning. Yes, it is possible that you will give your very life for the people you love. My wife gave her life, first to God and then to the people of Ecuador for thirty-one years. I may be called to do the same. But another meaning of the word "martyr" is to give your life away little by little as a witness for God. When I received Jesus as my Lord, one of my first prayers was to ask Him to spend my life like a dollar—one penny at a time, wherever He wanted. I was new to praying, but He still answered my prayer by using me for forty-five years around the world: twenty-two years in Ecuador, ten years in Uruguay, and as a witness everywhere, all the time.

I am asking you to do the same. Be God's witnesses as a T3D International disciple. Train other disciples to be used in a world that needs the power of the Trinity. When we ask for the Holy Spirit to fill you with His power, launch out immediately. Be a witness to the far corners of your world in His name. When we ask for the Trinity to fill our life, we will be His anointed witnesses in a dark world.

Chapter Fourteen:
"How" Do You Make a Disciple?

You have read the book. "How" does this book help you make a disciple? I want you to digest the information that has been given to you. This is an extra chapter to help you process what you have read. I am going to take time to quickly summarize the book chapter by chapter, highlighting some of the pertinent information so you know how to train at least three disciples. I do not want you to miss the teaching that you will need to duplicate your training for others. The purpose of this book was to give you structure (or handles to hold on to) to help alleviate your fear of making disciples. If you fear the process, you will never obey the Lord and train disciples.

I also want to note that Christ did not sit down and publish a book about how to make disciples. He walked for three years with a group of twelve men. Jesus shared life with these men—good and bad times, and times of joy and sadness. These men wrote down what they had seen and heard about the Yada of the Trinity. What we do not see in the New Testament is a discipleship format that the disciples used to gather and train their own group of disciples. What we do see is that disciples were continually trained. They were trained by the twelve original disciples and everyone who read about or saw the results of Jesus's training. Some received Jesus's ministry directly, and they instantly became His disciples. The process of developing an intimate relationship with an all-loving God took the full three years of Jesus's ministry and beyond.

The disciples' training was not consummated until they received the fullness of what the Trinity offered and learned that they were loved from the beginning of time. They also learned how to truly love others. These teachings are written in the New Testament and in the chapters of this book.

I want to show you three examples of the discipleship method Jesus used. First, look at the story of the woman at the well in John 4. Jesus crossed cultural boundaries to give a powerful testimony of His love for a lost soul. The woman tested Him as best she could, but she could not help falling in love with His teaching. She was convicted by Him. She incorporated the Yada of the Trinity and testified to her whole Samaritan town. They all believed in Christ. In this story, God's Word caused a town of culturally unaccepted people to believe and follow Jesus. I have also given you God's Word to go make disciples.

Another account of Jesus's discipleship is found in Mark 5, describing the man living in the tombs. Jesus freed the man personally with His words. Not everyone who saw and heard Jesus wanted to be His disciple, but the man who was freed did, and he wanted to be Jesus's disciple immediately. Jesus did not let the man physically follow Him. Instead, He told the man to go home and tell everyone about what He did and the mercy that He showed. All the people were amazed. They knew who the man used to be and saw that a free and merciful man was now speaking.

A third example can be found in John 9, where Jesus interacted with a man who was born blind. While the religious leaders debated who had sinned for this man to be blind, Jesus walked up and showed love. He healed the man in an unorthodox way, with mud and His spit. Now that method will mess with your theology! Please do not start this method as a tradition for healing blind eyes unless the Lord starts a healing ministry for you.

In all three cases, Jesus's love for the people gave them an encounter with the Trinity. In each case, the Trinity was represented by the Son. Each time, the reaction to the love, peace, and mercy of Jesus was to immediately tell someone else about Him. All three had a deep-seated joy and peace as they testified. Towns, groups, families, and individuals reacted to the testimonies and were excited to know Jesus too. Jesus is the core of the T3D International program; we are to spread the word about who He is. As we spread the gospel, we need to make Christ-followers: make disciples! I believe that we need to get excited about who He is. We need to make disciples who make disciples, who make disciples!

As I have been sharing, the Trinity wants to dismantle some of our deepest-held theologies so they can be reassembled to agree with a Trinitarian Biblical Theology. No, I do not want you to begin selling "spittle for the blind." I want you to be open to the many methods of loving and healing others. Many religious people did not question Jesus's methods, but instead questioned his religious cultural correctness. When the religious leaders questioned the blind man, he asked if the religious leaders wanted to be Jesus's disciples too. His faith was simple: I was blind and now I see. This is my story, too: I was lost and now I am found. The religious leaders recognized the man as Jesus's disciple. When Jesus returned to the man, the man did not recognize Jesus right away. But the man and others around him saw the kindness of Jesus and began to worship Him.

I have one final example of Jesus's discipleship to share with you. I want to mention Paul. Paul did not physically walk with Jesus. He saw Jesus in a vision. That vision turned Paul's life around. Before that encounter with Jesus, he was a murderer and hated everyone who followed Christ. Paul was raised and taught by the best teachers of Jewish theology.

It amazes me how much time the Trinity spent correcting Paul's "known" and accepted theologies. Paul once walked in one way, and after his vision, he began walking in another direction, following Jesus. This vision profoundly changed his life and ministry. God used Paul to write the majority of the New Testament. His life is perhaps the best example of what I am trying to say with my book. We need to upgrade our epistemology using the Bible and Yada experiences with the Trinity.

Through time, others learned how to be disciples by studying the written word. I want to emphasize that you, a modern-day disciple, follow the same Jesus as these first disciples. My book teaches specific theologies from the Bible that highlight the relationship the Trinity wants to have with you. I explained that it is important to Yada-know the Trinity, to have experiences with Him in an intimate relationship.

The first chapter of theology, found in Chapter Four, explained the meaning of theology and the word "epistemology." Theology is the study of God. Epistemology is a study of how we know what we know. Each of the theologies in this book began by explaining how each theology was a study of God. Chapter Four also showed you that the core of who we are today is based on what we learned from major institutions during your childhood. The first major institution was your family. You learned what you believe today through your family. This socialization occurred in the first years of your life. During this early period, you learned what you know to help you survive in your own culture for the rest of your life. You learned what you know as truth before you had the ability to refute any information.

My goal in this chapter was to confirm the correct things that you learned to survive in your culture. I also wanted to suggest that you may have learned things about who the Trinity is and to learned how the Trinity wants you to make disciples. It is possible that you did not learn those things. The purpose of this chapter was to give you a solid reason for exchanging what you learned as a child for a more informed truth that you learned as an adult. If you did not learn about the Trinity and discipleship in your formative years of epistemology, my task was to present biblical truth.

In this same chapter, you learned the importance of the core verse of T3D International: Matthew 28:19. You learned that this verse is a command of Jesus, endorsed by the Trinity, that may not have been given the prominence it was due throughout your early socialization. Training disciples is a command that is not being obeyed by many around the world. I used this chapter to encourage you to add to your adult epistemology. Keep on learning by using the Bible and having experiences with God. Influence others to do the same. My goal is to create a resurgence of the movement Jesus started by training disciples during His three years with them. I want you to train three disciples each, and have each of your disciples train disciples as well.

Chapter Five deepened your understanding of epistemology. More specifically, I taught you a new epistemology to be used in your adult life using the concepts Gnosis and Yada. This chapter was a combination of theology and epistemology. To make disciples, it is important to distinguish between Gnosis and Yada. If your early epistemology only allowed you to know "about" God (Gnosis), what you learned will not allow you to fully understand the riches of having an intimate relationship with Him (Yada.) You must maintain the Gnosis you have learned but add a Yada relational understanding of God.

An advantage you have as an adult is that you now have enough wisdom to evaluate what you learn so that you can continue to have an informed epistemology. As a youth, you simply accepted the information you were taught. The Bible is our best source for learning theology and the will of the Trinity. It is time to know about God (Gnosis) and to know Him personally (Yada). This chapter implores you to know God and the love He has for you. Transfer His love for you to others: make disciples. I taught you to evaluate what you learned as a child. Ask the Lord to continue teaching you both Gnosis and Yada. Pray to Him and ask Him to teach you His will so you can begin training others how to make disciples. Learn to teach others to have a healthy balance between Gnosis and Yada.

In Chapter Six, I explored a practical teaching: the idea that you need to be active in winning lost souls so you can train them as new disciples. It is important to train new disciples right away while they are fertile and are willing to accept the idea that they must train to be disciples and then train other disciples. Many wait too long. In this chapter, I gave you the scriptures you need to reach the lost and train both those who have served the Lord for years and those who have never made a convert how to evangelize. It is important to train both groups.

I gave you a simple structure to use for winning the lost to Jesus. The method I gave you is the Romans Road to Salvation. How does this chapter help you train disciples? The most obvious answer is that you need a steady stream of new converts to train as disciples. Some will desire to remain saved, and others will want to learn more about how to be Christ's disciple so they can obey Him and make others. The goal is not to fill the church with more people, but to make more disciples that will go out into the world!

A new convert with a heart filled with the peace of Jesus will always want to share the good news with a friend. If you make one convert and train them to be a disciple for Jesus, that disciple will learn to win others and make more disciples. Every new disciple will continue to duplicate the process that Jesus created. This chapter is full of practical tools for you and those you train. Be sure to take your time with the scriptures I presented. Use my free methods for memorizing these specific scriptures. I guarantee that the Holy Spirit will use what you hide in your heart at opportune moments.

Chapter Seven demonstrated how Jesus trained His disciples: He lived life with them. In this chapter, I showed how Jesus challenged the epistemologies of His disciples. They learned about God and knew of Him, but they did not know Him. This chapter also explores the deep love of the Trinity. The disciples saw how far the Trinity would go to express love to a crowd of people that others would not have cared for.

In the scriptures we studied in this chapter, Jesus met the crowd's basic need by serving dinner to twelve thousand men, women, and children. The disciples knew and trusted that Jesus could do something powerful, but their first reaction was human doubt rather than faith in the Trinity. This event was not only used to provide for the multitude, but also for Jesus to teach a new epistemology and further train His disciples. He wanted to teach and illustrate that the God of the Bible loved and cared for His creation in a powerful way.

You may have questions about how Jesus taught his disciples. We know that Jesus came to this earth as one hundred percent God and one hundred percent human. How can we train disciples like Jesus if we are merely human? I confess that this thought needs further research beyond my book. Here is my thought: As humans, we can trust the Trinity to do miracles through our lives just as Jesus did. Many believe that if a loved one needs healing, we can, by faith in the Trinity, pray for that healing. We see these types of miracles constantly in the Bible. Never be afraid to trust God. If His Word tells you to use His authority, then use His authority. This world needs to know that the Trinity of the Bible is real and loves His creation. You will see other chapters where questions like this may reappear. Ask yourself, if you trust the Trinity by faith, will you, according to the Bible, have results like Jesus? In John 14:12, Jesus said, "'Very truly I tell you, whoever believes in me will do the works I have been doing, and they will do even greater things than these, because I am going to the Father.'"

Chapter Eight was a theology of joy, teaching you how to do ministry with joy and live life with Jesus with joy. This chapter showed the sacrifices the disciples made to accomplish the plans of Jesus.

Sacrifices are still being made for the Lord today in our ministries. We must perform everything that we do for the Trinity with the joy of the Holy Spirit.

How did this chapter teach you "how" to make a disciple? This teaching is about how to train others while you maintain Jesus's joy. Even in tough times, be a real person, but exhibit that reality with His joy. Remember that a Christian is Christlike. A disciple is a follower of Christ. Paul said in 1 Corinthians 11:1, "Follow my example, as I follow the example of Christ."

Many people who have read the Bible for years have not realized that the disciples were filled with joy when they returned to give their account of ministry to Jesus. It must be a shock to read in Deuteronomy 28 that those who do not minister with joy will face severe consequences. I wrote this chapter on joy because of joy's importance to our identity as disciples. Teach your disciples about God's profound joy.

In Chapter Nine, I described three characteristics of God. As a disciple training other disciples, it is important to reveal the characteristics of God. We want to show that He is omniscient, omnipotent, and omnipresent. It is enough to say that your disciples need to be aware of His infinite power, infinite knowledge, and presence everywhere! There is no God like our Triune God! Chapter Nine is worth your disciples' involvement. Teach these three characteristics of the Trinity in a creative fashion.

Chapter Ten revealed a prayer that Jesus spoke privately to His Father. I believe that listening to His private prayer tells us a lot about what the Father, Son, and Holy Spirit thought about the Twelve original disciples—and what the Trinity thinks about your disciples today!

I believe that the Trinity wants us to listen in to this prayer. Though it was prayed over two millennia ago, it is still relevant today. We can learn a lot about what the Trinity thought about Jesus's disciples. We learned that the disciples' security was one of Jesus's primary concerns. We further learned that prayer extends to disciples today. Jesus's prayer is relative and relevant to your disciples both now and in the future.

Your disciples will train from a solid, biblical foundation of truth that will never be shaken. The world will always need the strength of the Trinity. Your disciples will benefit from this chapter when you teach them that they are important to Jesus. Those who pray from the heart to the Father love the ones they are praying for, because the recipient of our prayers is powerful enough to make a permanent difference. When disciples receive Jesus's kindness, they are more likely to reflect that same kindness in their lives, evangelism, and discipleship. This is why I had you list three people you want to disciple. Each day, you are to pray for those three disciples in the same way that Jesus did.

Chapter Eleven was the last theology that I taught: the theology of the "I Am" of Jesus. This is my favorite theology in the book. It not only confirms the prayer Jesus just prayed, but also illustrates Romans 5:8: He loves us so much that He demonstrated His love to us. Jesus saved His disciples from a near-death experience in an explosive situation as He won a decisive battle for the souls of humanity during the second battle in the garden. Remember, humanity lost the first battle in the Garden of Eden.

This chapter examined a moment of culmination in Christ's ministry. There were many individuals in the garden ready to take Jesus's life. The enemy was working behind the scenes to destroy the Trinity's eternal plan for the salvation of His creation. The battle lines were drawn between good and evil. How was this a chapter about how you can make a disciple? You must train your disciples to always trust the One who created them, who loves and protects them.

Chapter Twelve was important because it outlined how to complete the Social/Evangelistic Project. This project is of paramount importance to each disciple. These projects teach you to enact the Yada heart of God. Each disciple is obligated to help another in their local area in some way. Disciples are required to use their own funds and creative ideas.

It may not feel comfortable to complete this project because most people are concerned primarily with themselves. For someone to help another person in a way that will make a difference, the Trinity must explode in them from the inside out. This process is what Acts 1:8 is all about. God will use you to touch others. When you show true love to help another person and have no hidden agenda, you are showing the heart of God in a practical way.

I asked you to do the Social/Evangelistic Project as part of a team. It will be hard for one person to complete alone, but it will be easier if you can depend on the talents of other disciples. When this project is completed correctly, you will receive a Yada response. The recipient should ask, "Who is your God, and why are you doing this for me?" Do your project with genuine love. God's love is the only thing the enemy cannot duplicate.

Chapter Fifteen:
Benefits of Training with T3D International

My book centers on your relational interactions with the Trinity. We serve a relational God who lives with us and wants us to have an intimate relationship with Him and with our disciples. The process of making disciples will also bring benefits to your spiritual lives and to the Kingdom of God.

In this chapter, I want to list some of the benefits of training with the T3D International program. Some of these bullet points were written by previous students of my discipleship course; others are benefits that I hope you have experienced in your training. You may read this chapter if would like to see feedback from other disciples and be encouraged. Otherwise, you can skip to the final section of the book.

Here are some of my thoughts and the thoughts of past participants who shared how T3D has benefitted them.

Benefits to God

- He is blessed that you know His will and are enthusiastic to obey His will in Matthew 28:19: make disciples!
- God is pleased with your purposeful obedience.

Benefits to You

- Not many of those who studied T3D International were discipled when they accepted Jesus as their personal Savior. This study gave that discipleship teaching to each one, and now they will begin to make new disciples.
- Growth in the spiritual disciplines.
- T3D International demonstrates the meaning of Yada.
- Growth in deep biblical knowledge.

- Challenged to read His Word from Genesis to Revelation.
- You become interested in winning the lost.
- When Jesus asks how many disciples you have made, you will proudly answer Him.
- Learning T3D International makes you sensitive to Bible verses that describe the intimate, relational God.
- Makes students more aware of how God loves us and how we should love others.
- Makes me more aware of the need to pray for others.
- Makes me more aware of the personal needs of others.
- You are no longer a spectator but a trained participant.
- T3D disciples are aligning with God's will.
- Learning to see myself as God sees me, understanding that I can be used by Him no matter what age I am.
- T3D International helped me to break through my fears and limitations.
- Understanding the love of God helped me understand that no person is better than another.
- God made each of us diverse; I understand that we were created uniquely as originals for Him.
- Discipleship made me aware of God's true purpose for me in this world.
- T3D International teaching is a living experience that transformed my life and makes me participate in the reality of God's purpose for me.
- T3D International has led me to understand that I can be used by God to impact other people's lives by demonstrating God's love.
- The love of God is now reflected in my actions.
- T3D discipleship transformed my life and the lives of the people close to me.

- I have understood that I am unique and special to God and that the Trinity is not just another religion, a God who wants an intimate relationship.

- T3D International goes beyond sharing the Word of God. It allows us to see the spiritual and material needs of others.

- I learned to do intimate discipleship as Jesus did.

- T3D International material is very applicable, it is easy to understand, and it focuses on the idea that we depend on the Trinity.

- A deep relationship with God will mean that we stop being who we have learned to be to become who the Trinity wants us to be.

- When you buy the T-shirt for graduation, you identify with something bigger than yourself.

Benefits to Pastors and Churches

- Churches will be filled with new converts.

- Starting an authentic relationship with God and others by making disciples extended His Kingdom in our church.

- God will work supernaturally in a church when its members maintain an intimate relationship with Him.

- Barriers to carrying out the work of God alone are broken, and the work is distributed to everyone.

- T3D International challenges the members of the church to know and experience what their eyes cannot yet see.

- Churches are filled with new disciples.

- Churches now have a structure to reach others in their countries and other countries.

- Making disciples rather than making church members strengthens your church.

- The pastor who has disciples who make more disciples will be able to see healthy growth in his church.

- Like the scriptures, T3D can be contextualized and easily adapted in multiple countries.
- Many church members will be systematically trained as disciples.
- T3D International training adds a level of maturity to the church.
- Many groups of trained disciples are now interested in getting others outside the walls of the church to accomplish God's will.
- With T3D International training, many are now interested in completing the Great Commission.
- Fear of talking to others about Jesus is broken down.
- One pastor said his congregation came out of ignorance to know the truth about fulfilling the mandate of Matthew 28:19.
- T3D International encourages the church to teach others to get involved in the Kingdom of God.
- Not only adults are reached for Christ, but also young people.
- After T3D International training, the church learned that the work of the church is not done by just the pastor but is distributed to everyone.
- T3D-trained disciples have become leaders in the church.
- T3D has clearly taught us "how" to make a disciple.

Benefits to Non-Christians

- Social/Evangelistic projects completed by T3D International teams bless many communities.
- Non-Christians feel the love of God through the love of the church toward them personally. They see the church as alive and active.
- Non-believers will see an example of the love of Jesus through his disciples. They will receive relief and help in situations that they could not otherwise solve themselves.

The T3D Mission Fund and Merchandise Store

Thank you for reading my book! I had a lot of fun writing and teaching the material internationally. I pray it will be a benefit to you. Mostly, I want the Trinity to use you to make disciples around the world.

You have accomplished a great feat; you have read the entire book! Thank you so much for believing in what the Lord has placed in my heart. I do believe that the Trinity is crying out many truths to the world. One of those is that you need to make disciples!

I would like to give you two opportunities: one to support my mission, and one to purchase items from the T3D International merchandise store.

T3D International Mission Fund

If you would like to support me in teaching T3D International in Ecuador, Africa, Europe and the ends of the world, please help me with your prayers and finances. Prayers are very much appreciated, and I cannot do God's will without your prayers. Finances will help me with my airfare and the ability to stay in other countries while I teach.

If you desire to support my mission work with a one-time or monthly gift, you can use your phone to scan the QR code below. I have discovered that those who invest even a minimum have more of an appreciation for what they receive. The QR code will connect you directly to my mission account. The full amount sent through this QR code will be sent to me; nothing is taken out for administration fees.

Link to Dr. Mills's
Mission Fund

T3D International Merchandise Store

The T3D International merchandise store website is still under construction. If you are interested in purchasing a T-shirt or any other merchandise, contact Bryana Mills with this email: T3DiMerch@gmail.com. This store and its website will be further developed in the coming months. Currently, you can purchase T3D T-shirts, graduation diplomas (signed by Dr. Michael Mills), and the salvation scripture memory cards. Below is an example of the scripture cards.

T3D Romans Road Scripture Memorization Cards

When you buy your T3D International T-shirt after you complete the book, it will give you a sense of community with others around the world who have been trained with the same program. You are a part of something big that the Lord is doing around the world! Below is the design on the T-shirt.

The example shown is written in Spanish ("Soy Original"). The store has the logo in English as well. "Soy Original" means "I Am an Original." Here are the meanings of the tee shirt symbols. First, notice the DNA symbol. For us, that sign represents that God has put the ability to make disciples with His power into our DNA. If you take off the two tails of the DNA, you will see a drawing of a fish. In the time of the first disciples and the Roman persecution, you would be risking your life to say that you were a Christian. If you did not know if you were talking to a Christian, you would simply draw half the fish. If the other person responded by drawing the other line, completing a drawing of a fish, you knew that you were talking to another Christian. In the middle of the DNA logo, you notice a throne with a cross. For T3D International, this represents God's lordship in our lives. To the right of the logo is a fingerprint in a heart shape. The heart represents the Son and therefore (the Word). Notice the Trinity: Father, Son, and Holy Spirit in the logo.

Acknowledgements

Before I wrote this book, I made sure that the T3D International program functioned in various cultures. I want to thank the leaders in the order that I trained them.

In Uruguay, pastors Uber and Sole gave me my first fourteen church leaders to train. Those fourteen leaders turned into over eight hundred people that I trained across the entire country of Uruguay. I appreciate all eight hundred students for being the first to study T3D.

I trained four hundred pastors, leaders, and church members in Ecuador. The first group that I trained was in Atacames, Ecuador. I'd like to thank pastors Pepe and Charito and their incredible leaders who trained with me. Training this group enabled me to change the name from T3D to T3D International. While I trained leaders in Atacames, I also trained leaders in Quininde, Ecuador. Thank you, pastors Hugo and Soraya, and your incredible leaders.

I also used T3D International to train the church Cross of the Valley (La Cruz del Valle). Thank you to its pastors, Jimmy and Elba, and their daughters Dana and Keren. La Cruz trained simultaneously with the church Torre Fuerte, led by pastors Jacobo and Chave. I thank these pastors with their combined numbers of eighty leaders who trained for three months.

I also thank pastor Jessica Suarez from Guayaquil a leader of this strategic area for the Great Commission. She worked hard and organized many other pastors so that I was able to train one hundred sixty leaders over a six-month period.

I also want to thank Reina in Chattanooga, Tennessee, and Caroline in Kenya, Africa for studying T3D International on Zoom for three months.

I would like to thank Asbury Theological Seminary, and particularly the Beeson Scholarship Program. I directly experienced kindness from Asbury in 2004 when they gave me a full scholarship for my doctoral degree. In 1990, Ralph Beeson bequeathed over thirty-eight million dollars to create a center to train visionary pastors as they continued their education. His scholarship extended internationally to help working leaders. As a missionary to Ecuador, I was selected by the Beeson scholarship as a doctoral candidate. I am very thankful for Mr. Beeson's generosity, since the Trinity gave me the vision for T3D International during my studies at Asbury.

I want to thank my sister Keri for cleaning up my manuscript with her initial edits. Also, thank you Séan for your work to help me format my book. Both of you helped me tremendously.

Finally, I want to thank my editor, Selena Hostetler, for rescuing me with a deep revision of my material. Without your help, my book would not have been published in time. May the Lord bless you for helping me to state my heart's burden clearly and grammatically.

Bibliography

BibleTools. "Thayer's Greek Lexicon: Ginosko." Accessed July 23, 2023. https://www.bibletools.org/index.cfm/fuseaction/Lexicon.show/ID/G1097/ginosko.htm.

Hyles, Jack. "There Remaineth Yet Very Much Land to Be Possessed - Sunday Morning Sermon June 28, 1970." The Jack Hyles Home Page. Accessed July 23, 2023. https://www.jackhyles.com/muchland.htm.

Molnar, Paul D. "The Trinity and the Freedom of God." *Journal for Christian Theological Research* 8 (2003). https://digitalcommons.luthersem.edu/jctr/vol8/iss2003/1/.

Newman, Barclay Moon, and Eugene Albert Nida. *A Handbook on the Gospel of John.* United Bible Societies Handbooks. New York: United Bible Societies, 1993.

Schuller, Robert. *Facebook*, September 19, 2011. https://www.facebook.com/254517043904/posts/any-fool-can-count-the-seeds-in-an-apple-but-only-god-can-count-the-apples-in-on/10150338747923905/.

Sjogren, Steve. *Conspiracy of Kindness: A Unique Approach to Sharing the Love of Jesus.* Revised and Updated. Ada, Michigan: Baker Publishing Group, 2008.

Spence-Jones, H. D. M., ed. *The Acts of the Apostles.* Vol. 1. The Pulpit Commentary. London; New York: Funk & Wagnalls Company, 1909.

Thatcher, Jeff. "Nothing Stronger." Arkansas Online, July 22, 2023. https://www.arkansasonline.com/news/2021/sep/16/nothing-stronger/.

Vincent, Marvin Richardson. *Word Studies in the New Testament.* Vol. 2. New York: Charles Scribner's Sons, 1887.

Watch for Dr. Michael Séan Mills' next book:

A Wee Man:
Gave His Fleeting Life to the Lord, and the Lord Used It.

My next book is in the works, and I hope you will be blessed to read it. The Lord allowed me to do many miracles over my thirty-two years of ministry as a missionary. One example is when He made "construction sand" for me to use in the foundation of the five hundred-seat church I was building on San Cristobal Island in the Galapagos. I am excited to share this and many other miracles.

To stay updated on its release date, email me with "A Wee Man" in the subject line at *Visionary4God@gmail.com*.

Made in United States
Troutdale, OR
11/02/2024

24372058R00124